WHEN RIGHT IS WRONG

10-22-01

Wayne, thanks for a wonderful interview. We look forward to seeing you and Doty both in Valpo.

Hank &
Deb Moratz

HOW TO ORDER THIS BOOK

BY PHONE: 800-233-9936 or 717-291-5609, 8AM–5PM Eastern Time

BY FAX: 717-295-4538

BY MAIL: Order Department
Technomic Publishing Company, Inc.
851 New Holland Avenue, Box 3535
Lancaster, PA 17604, U.S.A.

BY CREDIT CARD: American Express, VISA, MasterCard

PERMISSION TO PHOTOCOPY–POLICY STATEMENT

Authorization to photocopy items for internal or personal use, or the internal or personal use of specific clients, is granted by Technomic Publishing Co., Inc. provided that the base fee of US $3.00 per copy, plus US $ .25 per page is paid directly to Copyright Clearance Center, 222 Rosewood Drive, Danvers, MA 01923, USA. For those organizations that have been granted a photocopy license by CCC, a separate system of payment has been arranged. The fee code for users of the Transactional Reporting Service is 1-56676/95 $5.00 + $ .25.

WHEN RIGHT IS WRONG

Fundamentalists and the Public Schools

Richard P. Manatt, Ph.D.
Professor of Education and Program Coordinator
Educational Administration
College of Education
Iowa State University

LANCASTER · BASEL

When Right is Wrong
a TECHNOMIC®publication

Published in the Western Hemisphere by
Technomic Publishing Company, Inc.
851 New Holland Avenue, Box 3535
Lancaster, Pennsylvania 17604 U.S.A.

Distributed in the Rest of the World by
Technomic Publishing AG
Missionsstrasse 44
CH-4055 Basel, Switzerland

Copyright ©1995 by Technomic Publishing Company, Inc.
All rights reserved

No part of this publication may be reproduced, stored in a
retrieval system, or transmitted, in any form or by any means,
electronic, mechanical, photocopying, recording, or otherwise,
without the prior written permission of the publisher.

Printed in the United States of America
10 9 8 7 6 5 4 3 2 1

Main entry under title:
   When Right is Wrong: Fundamentalists and the Public Schools

A Technomic Publishing Company book
Bibliography: p.
Includes index p. 145

Library of Congress Catalog Card No. 94-61497
ISBN No. 1-56676-222-7

*To my son Joel Price Manatt
who understands what this
book is about*

TABLE OF CONTENTS

Acknowledgements xi

Chapter 1. School Culture Wars: The Background 1
  The Attack on Public Schools   2
  A Label for the Protesters   3
  The Battle Lines   4
  The Most Common Targets   5
  School Reform Spawns Outcome-Based Education   8
  Problems with OBE   11
  The Rise of Christian Fundamentalism   12
  Fundamentalism Won't Die   13
  GOP Allies in Conflict   17
  Coalition to Fight Back   19
  Should Fundamentalists Opt Out?   21
  What Will Happen to the Public Schools?   22
  Endnotes   22
  References   23

Chapter 2. The Attack on "Government Schools" Blunts School Reform 27
  What's Wrong?   28
  The Roots of the Religious Right   31
  Educators' Loose Language   32
  The Christian Coalition   34
  How Can the Religious Right Believe These Things?   37
  Attending a Religious Right Seminar   38

A Change in Tactics   45
One Superintendent Fights Back   49
Preparation Tips   57
Endnotes   58
References   59

Chapter 3. Why Are the Fundamentalists So Unhappy with Public Schools? 61
What Do They Want?   63
Factors in the Fray   66
Conclusions   77
Endnotes   79
References   79

Chapter 4. Seeking a Middle Ground for School Reform 81
The Reforms   83
The Goals   85
World-Class Schools   91
Outcome-Based Education   93
Opposition to School Change   103
What to Do?   106
Censorship over Charges of New Age
  Religion and Satanism   114
Multiculturalism and Globalism   116
AIDS, Premarital Sex, and Condoms   117
Endnotes   120
References   121

Chapter 5. Survival and Victory in the School Culture Wars 123
Fundamentalists' Strategy   124
Beliefs of Fundamentalists   128
Home Schooling   130
Lessons from Littleton, Colorado; Adrian,
  Michigan; and Kentucky   131

Kentucky Educational Reform Act (KERA) 135
Misinformation and the Biggest Hoax 136
A Plan for Victory in the Schools' Culture Wars 139
Endnotes 142
References 142

Index 145

ACKNOWLEDGEMENTS

I am grateful to the colleagues who have provided research tips, publications, and news clippings, as well as taking time to read and comment on portions of the draft: Frances Kayona, Jennifer Brookins, Dianna Mitchell, Gary Schnellert, Katy and Alan Rice, Jim Sweeney, Charles Railsback, Ralph Woodward, and Barbara Licklider. Alan "Butch" Rice also spent a year listening to right-wing talk show hosts to keep me informed.

For timely advice and a blizzard of faxed tidbits, I am deeply indebted to *International Journal of Educational Reform* editor Fenwick English and his wife Betty Steffy. Heartfelt thanks are due to typists Carol Wessinger, Janet Roby, Renae La Cosse, and Marla Smith. Most of all, I am thankful to my research associate, Frances Kayona, and my wife Jackie who, as usual, were deeply involved throughout this writing project.

CHAPTER 1
School Culture Wars: The Background

Congress shall make no law respecting an establishment of religion, or prohibiting the free exercise thereof; or abridging the freedom of speech, or of the press, or the right of the people peaceably to assemble, and to petition the Government for a redress of grievances.[1]

THE battle between the Religious Right and the public schools did not begin with Madalyn Murray O'Hair single-handedly removing God, the Bible, and prayer from public schools in 1962 (Americans United, 1993)! The arguments over how to maintain Jefferson's wall of separation between church and state actually predate the Constitution. The framers wrote the Constitution as a secular document not because they were hostile to Christianity, but because they did not want to imply that the new federal government had any authority to meddle in religion.

The two "religious activities" school cases of the 1960s did provide a watershed point for many Fundamentalists' concern for the public schools and should be revisited briefly to provide a background for the ensuing chapters of this book.

Outspoken atheist leader Madalyn Murray O'Hair played no role in the Supreme Court's school prayer decision in 1962. In this case, *Engel v. Vitale,* the United States Supreme Court ruled 8–1 against New York's Regents' prayer, a "nondenominational" prayer that state education officials had comprised for public school students to recite. The state-sponsored devotion was chal-

---

[1] Amendment I to the Constitution of the United States of America. The first ten Amendments (Bill of Rights) were ratified effective December 15, 1791.

lenged in court by a group of parents from New Hyde Park. Some parents were atheists; some were believers. Ms. O'Hair was never involved in this case.

In 1963, Ed Schempp, a Philadelphia area resident, brought a case to the Supreme Court, challenging mandatory Bible reading in Pennsylvania's schools. At about the same time, O'Hair was challenging Bible reading, as well as the recitation of the Lord's Prayer, in Maryland public schools. The Supreme Court consolidated the cases (and used only Schempp's name, much to O'Hair's dismay). The Court ruled 8–1 that devotional Bible reading or other government-sponsored religious activities in public schools are unconstitutional.

> The *Engel* and *Schempp* cases were a result of the changing religious landscape of the United States. As religious minorities grew more confident of their rightful place in American society, they came to resent the *de facto* Protestant flavor in many public schools. Litigation was inevitable. The high court's rulings striking down mandatory prayer and devotional Bible reading in public schools would have occurred if O'Hair had never been born. The controversial Texas atheist serves as a convenient villain for Religious Right propagandists who hate religious liberty and church-state separation. (Americans United, 1993, p. 13)

THE ATTACK ON PUBLIC SCHOOLS

Public schools are supposed to be free of sectarian control, but Religious Right groups and their local affiliates are conducting an unrelenting campaign of harassment and intimidation against public education all over the nation.

The Religious Right's biggest bogey man, the public schools, has been accused by politically aggressive Christian Fundamentalists of everything from promoting secular humanism and "new age" philosophies to practicing witchcraft and mind control (Boston, 1994, p. 4).

Serious scholars (and the courts) can't find much evidence to support these charges. The Fundamentalists depend on a variety of semantic tricks to justify their criticisms. Goals 2000 and

Outcome-Based Education (OBE) are both considered similar conspiracies to destroy family values; any story that deals with witches, or even Barney, promotes *witchcraft!* Public schools are no good, but any curriculum revisions that do not hawk their narrow brand of ultraconservative Christianity are, by default, "antireligious" or "humanistic."

> Many observers who monitor the Religious Right believe the movement has an ambitious, long range goal in mind through these attacks. Ultimately, the Religious Right hopes to turn Americans against non-sectarian public education and move the country toward a system of taxpayer supported private religious schools. (Boston, 1994, p. 4)

Such a goal is long term; in the short term Religious Right leaders want to Christianize the public schools and take them over if possible. Their various publications use language such as "... especially suited Christians should pray and work tirelessly to obtain teaching, school board, and even administrative posts within public education." "The attitude and approach of Christians should be that they should never expose their children to public education, but they should work increasingly to expose public education to the claims of Christ."

Jerry Falwell wrote in his 1979 book, *America Can Be Saved,* "I hope I live to see the day when, as in the early days of our country, we won't have any public schools. The churches will have taken over again and Christians will be running them. What a happy day that will be."

A LABEL FOR THE PROTESTERS

Deciding what to call religious conservatives who have become so vocal and visible in their dissatisfaction with the public schools is a dilemma. Steven Bates (1993), in writing *Battleground,* settled on the term *Fundamentalists.* This term was first used to describe American Protestants eighty-five years ago. At that time it described peaceful, if a bit weird, Christians. Now Fundamentalist, unfortunately, conjures up thoughts of TWA jetliners filled with hostages, car bombs, and the World Trade Center. Some writers use the term *Religious Right;* others prefer to address the "againers" as the New Christian Right or Conservative Christians. Evangelicals include some religious conservatives who are politically liberal. In this book I will use *Fundamentalists* as the umbrella term but will also use the other common labels as they are appropriate for the particular incident being described. Whatever the label, no offense is intended.

THE BATTLE LINES

The United States is experiencing a major curriculum battle; many would call it a war. It's probably a very desirable and defining event in our educational and social history. Educational leaders are struggling nationwide to know how to improve our schools enough to meet the challenges of the twenty-first century and our economic competitors in Europe and the Pacific Rim. Suddenly, it seems to them, critics are everywhere: critics who run for school boards as stealth candidates; critics who flood the hearing halls when state legislators consider educational goals; and critics who are ever so skillful at using half-truths and out-of-context quotes from educational research to counter any suggestions of change from direct, intensive instruction in phonics and the basics. When it appeared that an amendment to H.R. 6 (the companion piece to Goals 2000) would require all teachers to have state certification in their assigned subjects, 800,000 calls flooded the Congressional switchboards in a successful lobbying effort to "avoid this death sentence to home schooling and private schools."

In the ensuing chapters we will examine the past five years and discover how the Fundamentalists have had their high hopes of the Reagan years be dampened by four years of Bush and dashed by the election of Clinton. Values, teaching methods, content, and, especially, multiculturalism have continued to be the points of disagreement. The Religious Right wants no values taught when it is fighting diversity but wants values taught when it proposes character development "based on traditional concepts of right and wrong, such as honesty, integrity, selflessness, compassion and self-discipline."

The civil war over values has the liberal, moderate, and mainline thinkers in education charging that if any self-esteem or ethnic pride materials are removed under right-wing pressure, it's *censorship*. On the other hand, the People for the American Way will insist that right-wing censors are pushing the public schools back to the dark ages with an approach that tells students *what* to think instead of teaching them *how* to think. Nancy Reagan's advice to young people, "Just say no," is an oft mentioned example. In actual practice, schools are always teaching students what to think. Even a short chat with most high school seniors will elicit a wealth of stories about social studies teachers who have a very "personal" approach to economics, government, and even geography. Generally speaking, social studies teachers are liberals, Democrats, and social activists. This, of course, is not to say that only social studies instructors teach values. All teachers promote the knowledge of their subjects, along with punctuality, accuracy, obedience, self-discipline, cooperation, and hard work.

Schools teach many concepts in a very one-sided manner. Racial equality is taught without mention of Malcom X's beliefs about Jews or William Shockley's theories of genetics. The Iowa Curriculum Guides have promoted soil conservation over short-term profits since the 1930s, California textbook guides say that "the practice of thrift must be encouraged," and Tennessee schools must teach "the contribution of black people to the history and development of this country and the world." Imagine what would happen if "spend it quick" or the "burden of black people" were used as values!

THE MOST COMMON TARGETS

To counter the charge of the Fundamentalists requires that educators, parents, and their moderate allies know the most common targets for attack. From their national headquarters Pat Robertson, Phyllis Schlafly, Donald Wilmon, Robert Simonds, and others manipulate an army of followers who, in turn, make life miserable for public school teachers and administrators. The targets include

1. *Outcome-Based Education*—Known to educators as a powerful school transformation plan, it requires that students demonstrate proficiency in certain aspects of the subject before moving on to more advanced topics or graduating. The Religious Right sees OBE as a "new secular humanism." In some states, educators have been accused by the Religious Right of engaging in social engineering by requiring students to exhibit certain predetermined attitudes, such as respect for other cultures and diversity.

2. *Sex education*—Courses in human growth and development, physical education, and health must include sex education in an era of AIDS and runaway illegitimate births. Nonetheless, Religious Right activists demand that public schools drop any reference to contraception, abortion, or homosexuality.

   Fundamentalists frequently urge that the "just say no" approach be used. The program they prefer is abstinence-based and goes by the title of "Sex Respect." Sex Respect was developed by a Roman Catholic activist and has been found by a state judge in Louisiana to contain medically inaccurate content.

3. *Censorship of curricula or books*—Educators are familiar with the Fundamentalists' attack on specific books, usually those containing profanity or sexual overtones. *Catcher in the Rye* by Salinger is a typical target. In recent years, however, the Religious Right attacks entire programs and curricula. They are particularly unhappy with antidrug courses designed to keep students free of illegal narcotics and alcohol by boosting self-esteem. The overall motivation behind these attacks is unclear. Why would Fundamentalists attack efforts to reduce the use of alcohol? Many scholars of the Religious Right believe it centers on the likelihood that "thinking for yourself" undermines "parental authority."

   The most commonly attacked programs are

   - *Impressions,* a reading series that contains a small

percentage of stories containing fantasy themes. The charge from the Fundamentalists—"witchcraft!"
- *Pumsey,* a series of stories about a dragon puppet whose purpose is to teach children self-respect and respect for others. The Religious Right claims that the stories teach "New Age religion and Hinduism." Their theory is that children are put into a "semi-sleepy state during which religious brainwashing takes place." Fundamentalists charge that Pumsey's phrase "I am me and I am enough" teaches youngsters they don't have to rely on God.
- *Quest,* developed by the United States Lion's Club, an antidrug program used in elementary and secondary schools. Again, Fundamentalists charge that the program weakens parental authority via occultism, values clarification, and psychotherapeutic techniques.

4. *Creationism*—Despite the Supreme Court ruling of 1987 that public schools may not require the teaching of creationism, Fundamentalists have not given up. According to Eugenie Scott of the National Center for Science Education in Berkeley, California, creationists have successfully created a climate of confusion and intimidation that has convinced many public schools to water down the teaching of evolution from public school science classes. They have also intimidated textbook publishers to the extent that many biologists agree that high school texts are inaccurate regarding evolution (Boston, 1994, p. 9).
5. *Equal access clubs*—Public high schools are required to allow student-led religious clubs to meet during noninstructional time if other noncurricular clubs are permitted to meet. The Equal Access Act was passed by Congress in 1984 and upheld by the Supreme Court in 1990. Pat Robertson's American Center for Law and Justice (ACLJ) [1] has charged that widespread abuses of the Act exist and has asked Attorney General Janet Reno and Education Secretary Richard Riley to intervene.
6. *Proselytism*—Both teachers and students are guilty of pros-

elytizing. Literature distribution by students; flag pole prayers at the start of the school year; teaching about the "cultural" aspects of Thanksgiving, Christmas, and Easter; and student-initiated prayer can all be subtle or not-so-subtle attempts to win converts.

SCHOOL REFORM SPAWNS OUTCOME-BASED EDUCATION

The problems of American public education seem so great that the public, parents, and politicians want someone to blame, somebody to hold accountable. Teachers, it is said, should be accountable in terms of students' academic achievement; school boards and administrators are asked for organizational accountability; state and federal political leaders are expected to be fiscally accountable.

An increasingly popular, albeit controversial, way to obtain greater accountability from teachers for their students' academic achievement is Outcome-Based Education (OBE). The state of Minnesota's Department of Education defines outcome-based education as a learner-centered, results-oriented system founded on the belief that all individuals can learn. In this system,

1. What is to be learned is clearly identified.
2. Learners' progress is based on demonstrated achievement.
3. Multiple instructional and assessment strategies are available to meet the needs of each learner.
4. Time and assistance are provided for each learner to reach maximum potential (Minnesota Department of Education, 1991).

The Educational Commission of the States reported in 1994 that twenty states had a results-oriented approach to educational standards.

William Spady, the key advocate of outcome-based education, has taken great pains to explain that OBE is not a program, but a way of designing, developing, delivering, and evaluating instructions in terms of its intended goals.

"From my perspective it means having *all* students learn well, not just the fastest, the brightest or the most advantaged. Unfortunately, our educational systems, schools and instructional programs are not organized to achieve or ensure successful results, instead they are organized primarily for student custody and administration convenience" (Spady, 1988, p. 40).

OBE supporters believe that all students can learn if given the time and support to do so. Another tenet of OBE is that success encourages success and that schools both create and control the conditions for success. When an outcome-based philosophy is followed in instructional design, *learning* is the constant and time is the variable, not vice versa. Critics of OBE, especially the Fundamentalists, don't believe that William Spady's concept is only a way of designing and delivering instruction. They believe it is a *program,* a program that is part and parcel of Goals 2000.

N. W. Hutchings (1994), writing in the monthly newsletter of his Southwest Radio Church, *The Prophetic Observer,* said,

> The so-called Goals 2000 bill guarantees that children will start to school ready to learn; no drugs or violence in schools; almost all students graduating with high scholastic grades and achievements. This means more federal control of education, and the only way the federal bureaucracy can guarantee more graduates with higher grades is Outcome-Based Education. [Hutchings continues with what he considers proof of a long-term conspiracy.]
>
> Goals 2000 will fulfill socialistic, atheistic, and one-world plans from John Dewey down to the present time. This is something the humanists have been working for since the turn of the century. Outcome-Based Education is part of the plan. A letter dated July 27, 1984, from G. Leland Burningham, Utah State Superintendent of Public Instruction, to T. H. Bell, U.S. Department of Education Secretary, stated in part:
>
> "I am forwarding this letter to accompany the proposal which you recommended Bill Spader [sic] and I prepare in connection with Outcome-Based Education. This proposal centers around the detailed process by which we will work together to implement Outcome-Based Education using research verified programs. This will make it possible to put Outcome-Based Education in place, not only in Utah but in all schools of the nation. . . . We sincerely urge your support for funding the proposal as presented."
>
> Goals 2000 (along with Outcome-Based Education) is federal intervention into the local school system, lock, stock, and barrel, including curriculums. (p. 2)

Part of the confusion rests with the combination of two components that comprise OBE. One is known as "competency-based education," a generic term for efforts aimed at defining and evaluating student performance. The other component is "mastery learning," a form of "individualized" instruction in which students are allowed the time necessary to master each unit of curriculum before moving to the next unit. "In essence, mastery learning is an instructional *process*. It involves organizing instruction, providing students with regular feedback on their learning progress, giving guidance and direction to help students correct their individual learning difficulties, and providing extra challenges for students who have mastered the material" (Guskey, 1985).

Obviously, OBE and mastery learning are not synonymous; however, most teachers who profess to have implemented OBE also employ mastery learning techniques. Indeed, to believe that all individuals can learn and that time is the important variable determining success would demand that a reasonable teacher give each learner "more than one chance to demonstrate that he or she has learned." Towers (1994) argues that "In essence, mastery learning is often times the engine that propels OBE programs. From recent testimonials it's an engine that propels well, although most reports are found in popular journals, not peer-reviewed scientific journals [2].

The mastery model derives its theoretical base from the work of John Carroll (1963) at Harvard and its popularity from Ben Bloom (1974, 1976, 1981), Fred Keller (1968), and Madeline Hunter (1985). Mastery learning is predicated on Carroll's idea of *time on task*. It requires

1. Dividing the learning into structural, hierarchical, sequential units of material
2. Providing clear instructional objectives
3. Dividing subject matter into short, individualized, incremental units
4. Individualized evaluation and monitoring of individual student progress

Contrary to popular belief, teachers who incorporate mastery learning into their teaching can continue to teach the same information and ideas, continue to lecture, form small discussion groups, and assign projects. They must, however, modify the way they do these activities in order to assure a high level of mastery for each student.

Frequently administered diagnostic assessments are critical to mastery learning. Teachers (or even entire school systems) develop and administer brief tests to determine the students' mastery of the daily objectives. The materials and skills are arranged in ever-increasing levels of complexity. The mastery model is based on a diagnostic notion of teaching in which the teacher diagnoses needs, then teaches to those needs, then tests, and then reteaches if necessary. When students master the skills and concepts, they proceed to the next level. Bloom claimed that 85 to 95 percent of all learners can master content and skills if given appropriate instructional time.

Five-to-ten question tests are used to determine students' mastery of the daily objectives. Generally, students who answer 15 percent of more incorrectly go over the work again until they achieve mastery. Students who need "correctives" are given individual work such as special reading, worksheet assignments, computer games, peer tutoring, small-group study sessions, group games, or other forms of cooperative learning.

Students who get the material right the first time (either in a pretest or in the first learning) are given "enrichments" that allow them to study the content more comprehensively. In mastery learning, students compete against their own record, not other students; thus, grading is not competitive, and many, if not all, can earn A's.

Benjamin Bloom's version of mastery learning has the teacher teach the unit to the whole class. A variation in which students work through the units independently is very common in vocational training and at the college level. The most widely used individualized format is the Personalized System of Instruction (PSI) developed by Fred Keller (1968).

PROBLEMS WITH OBE

OBE does take a tremendous amount of effort and structure to launch, K–12. Remember, it does little good for a third grade teacher to strive for mastery when her fourth grade counterpart is emphasizing "coverage." Even when curricula are redesigned, aligned with national standards, and have the appropriate assessments ready, the teachers are still required to further individualize their instruction, carry out a variety of remediation and enrichment activities on a daily basis, create and administer assessment tools, and keep a detailed record of each student's progress.

Second, OBE, when combined with master learning, demands that slower students be retaught if they don't meet the expected level of achievement on their first, second, third, or subsequent tries. The opposite is also true, i.e., when students meet the minimum competency expected on the first try, they should be given enrichment. This all seems very even-handed and desirable. In actual practice, however, remediation always seems to take precedence over enrichment activities. This is especially true when teachers' time is studied. A student is "enriched" once, but many correctives must be prepared.

Outcome-based education also turns the "sorting and selection process" on its ear. All students know they will have more than one chance "to show they have learned." Some students don't bother to study for the initial test, knowing full well they would always have another chance later. Grades don't mean as much because D's and F's on the initial test eventually turn into B's or better when the student reaches the minimum competency level. Critics view this aspect of OBE as a disaster; supporters say, "It's about time we quit worshiping grades!" Conservatives Rush Limbaugh and Phyllis Schlafly charge that this element of OBE will result in the "dumbing down of America."

THE RISE OF CHRISTIAN FUNDAMENTALISM

Christian Fundamentalism began around the turn of the century. To religious conservatives the Bible was law. As liberals began to loosen their interpretation of scripture, conservatives headed in the other direction. In 1895 the Niagara Bible Conference reduced Christian belief to five points, each based on the belief in the inerrancy (infallibility) of the Bible. Four of the points concerned Jesus, viz., the Virgin Birth and divinity, "substitutionary atonement" by which the Crucifixion atoned for the sins of others, the bodily resurrection, and the future return to earth. Religious conservatives of the time believed that their list would separate the true believers from all others.

Next, a pair of wealthy businessmen brothers from Los Angeles financed the Los Angeles Bible Institute. This organization bankrolled the publication and dissemination of a series of tracts written by conservative theologians exploiting the five points. The series was called *The Fundamentalists: A Testimony to the Truth*. In addition to advocating a very narrow interpretation of scripture, *The Fundamentalists* took great glee in attacking Mormons, Christian Scientists, and Roman Catholics. *The Fundamentalists* was immensely popular; three million copies were distributed from 1910 to 1915, and conservative Protestants were soon known as Fundamentalists.

Fundamentalists worked hard to obtain the passage of the Eighteenth Amendment (Prohibition) in 1919 and to stop the spread of the teaching of evolution in the public schools. "John Barley Corn" was another name for the devil! If the Bible couldn't be trusted on creation, they reasoned, it couldn't be trusted on salvation or anything else.

FUNDAMENTALISM WON'T DIE

Religious Fundamentalists continue to raise broad and difficult questions each time they challenge new textbooks, new approaches to curriculum, or programs that purport to teach values and character. They want the biblical story of creation taught as scientific fact. They keep coming back, decade after decade.

How can this be? The Scopes "monkey trial" seems like ancient history to most. Clarence Darrow made William Jennings Bryan and the Fundamentalists look like fools in his defense of John T. Scopes. True, Scopes was found guilty of violating the Tennessee law against teaching evolution in 1925. [The conviction was later overturned (*Scopes v. State,* 1927).] Nonetheless, in the press the Fundamentalists suffered a stunning defeat. Their cause was made to look foolish. How can you reason with people who don't believe in fossils? Was the world really created in six days?

Other setbacks followed, not the least of which was the repeal of Prohibition. From 1933 to the early 1960s the idea of legislating morality seemed discredited. More and more Protestant leaders adjusted to Darwinism, leaving Fundamentalists isolated.

During these years, public school educators continued to inculcate religion, but they did so in a nonsectarian manner. Classroom religion centered on the Bible. The day opened with a Bible passage, and often the students recited a prayer, typically the Lord's Prayer.

During three decades, the 1930s, 1940s, and 1950s, Fundamentalists remained largely detached from politics. All of this was to change with the 1962 Supreme Court ruling in the *Engel v. Vitale* case. Writing for the majority, Justice Hugo Black concluded from the facts in the New York case that "it is no part of the business of government to compose official prayers."

Ending prayer in public schools provided the spark that set off a firestorm of posturing, preaching, and defiant moves by politicians. Senator Robert Byrd of West Virginia castigated the justices for "tampering with America's soul." Governor George Wallace thundered that any Alabama school that dropped its religious exercises could "kiss its state aid good-bye." In Texas, where few school districts had an official position on religious exercises when the two prayer cases came down, nearly 90 percent of Texas districts required daily prayers a few years later.

Interestingly, the liberal magazine *The New Republic* foresaw the potential awakening of the radical right, which would be caused by the 1962 ruling. The magazine said that the Court had provided a rallying cry for religious-minded people and, in particular, among those Fundamentalist groups already attracted to the gospel "according to John Birch!"

Motivated by the school prayer ban, the Fundamentalist preachers took to politics as well as lawyers do. Jerry Falwell credits the school prayer decision for causing him to lead the

Moral Majority. Tim LaHaye argues that mailing his book, *Battle for the Mind*, free to thousands of Fundamentalist preachers, may have played a part in the Reagan landslide in 1980.

Tim LaHaye became the Religious Right's leading interpreter of secular humanism. LaHaye's detractors claim that "defining secular humanism is like trying to nail Jell-O to a tree." In his broadest definition LaHaye claims, "There isn't a nickel's worth of difference between a secular humanist and a liberal." He insists that "humanism is the greatest danger facing our nation today." "Humanism is responsible for the dreadful increase in venereal disease in our country, the rise of sexual perversion, the aborting of millions of babies, the escalating crime rate, and practically every social evil facing our society today." Indeed, he charges, "Behind each social problem in America, we will find a secular humanist thinker or theorist."

Harvard theologian Harvey Cox has observed that Fundamentalists don't insist that everyone adopt their religious beliefs, though that would no doubt gratify them. Instead, they seek to impose social norms or even legal ones, if possible, to make everyone behave like a Fundamentalist. American society used to impose such norms, Fundamentalists think, but progress and modernity have pushed the nation from its rightful path.

Secular humanism encompasses all of the changes that the radical right abhors: the new rules concerning sex (premarital sex, homosexuality, abortion, pornography), gender (feminism), signs of laxity toward communism, the decline of Biblical morality, the acceptance of the theory of evolution, and the diminution of religion in public life.

The original Scopes trial was almost seventy years ago, but as recently as 1985, East Tennessee Fundamentalists tried to force their beliefs into the Hawkins County School District. Vicki Frost and a few parent allies discovered "secular humanism" in the new textbooks. They charged that the county's textbook adoptions promoted witchcraft, rebellion, pacifism, and Hinduism. They went so far as to say that reading the books might even invite demonic possession. When the school board refused to drop the offending textbooks, the parent protesters filed suit in federal court (*Mozart v. Hawkins County Public Schools*, 1985).

Immediately, powerful interest groups joined the fray on each side. The small town textbook argument became big time news. The People for the American Way (PAW) supported the Hawkins County School Board. Concerned Women for America supported and advised Vicki Frost and her fellow plaintiffs.

At the first federal court level, the plaintiffs won. Judge Thomas Hull wrote that the plaintiffs believed that "after reading the entire Holt series a child might adopt the views of a feminist, a humanist, a pacifist, an anti-Christian, a vegetarian or an advocate of 'one-world government.'" The plaintiffs convinced the judge that their religious beliefs "compel them to refrain from exposure to the Holt series." Yet the school board had made reading the books a condition of obtaining a free public education. Because the plaintiffs were put to a choice between enjoying a public benefit and living by their faith, this was clearly in line with precedents, Hull ruled. The plaintiffs' religious rights were violated.

Hull's decision was later reversed, but the immediate response to the ruling was enlightening. "All I can say is praise God." wrote Beverly (Mrs. Tim) LaHaye in a fund-raising letter. But she went on to warn against a letdown of efforts and financial support. She said People for the American Way and Norman Lear's 150 high-powered lawyer staff would appeal.

At the same time PAW mailed a fund-raising letter that said "Scopes II" will continue and claimed that the issues were much more serious than in the original monkey trial. This time it's not just one teacher and the issue of evolution. This time, according to PAW, the Religious Right is attempting to force one intolerant version of God's law on everyone.

What can be learned from such a case? Steven Bates (1993) chronicled Vicki Frost's case in his thoughtful and even-handed book, *Battleground: One Mother's Crusade, the Religious Right and the Struggle for Control of Our Classrooms*. Bates believes that the Hawkins County Fundamentalists raised profound and difficult questions. How should a secular, tolerant state cope with devout but intolerant citizens in both public schools and in public life? How much control should parents have over their children's education? How should the public schools handle religious topics and religious students (Bates, 1993)?

GOP ALLIES IN CONFLICT

When the Fundamentalists picked school reform as a target of their attacks, it pitted business leaders against conservative social activists. Together, these two groups helped elect Ronald Reagan and George Bush president. They have a good chance at unseating Bill Clinton and recapturing the Congress. This continued alliance is necessary to the Republicans.

The educational policy debates in a number of states have seen moderate and conservative Republicans simultaneously fighting over control of the state party. They also see school reform much differently. Grass-roots activists, many with strong beliefs centering on traditional family values and religion, see school reforms that stress broader educational outcomes as a mistake. They want course requirements in Carnegie Units and acquisition of specific academic knowledge.

Business leaders, on the other hand, focus on the big picture of ill-prepared students and a changing economy. "Business doesn't really understand," says Jeanne Allen, president of the Washington-based Center for Education Reform and a former policy analyst for the conservative Heritage Foundation. "They hear people talk about higher-order thinking skills and they really believe that means children achieve at higher levels!" "Instead you get state laws and state outcomes that say things like children will learn to reason better and cope with stress without ever dealing with what they will learn in math, science, or history," Ms. Allen charges (Harp, 1994, p. 12).

Kevin Poston, a spokesman for the National Alliance of Business, reports that a recent unpublished survey of his group indicates that business leaders are frustrated with resistance to school changes. "They don't understand what the problem is," Poston said. "We are talking about standards and focusing on what kids are learning. What is so odious about setting outcomes and standards for kids (Harp, 1994, p. 12)?

The Chamber of Commerce, the National Alliance of Business, and other business groups were key allies in helping the Clinton administration pass the Goals 2000: Educate America Act and the companion School-to-Work legislation.

As the new programs are implemented, the clashes between

the reform supporters and opponents could become incendiary. Deanna Duby, director of education policy for People for the American Way, a civil liberties group that has worked to counter conservative education activists, predicts that this will be the hottest issue going in education in 1994 and 1995.

Interestingly, the Fundamentalists agree that a battle is underway, but they are not willing to accept the notion that they are spreading it.

> "The cultural war has been presented as the religious right invading the world of politics, when nothing could be more wrong," said Paul Hetrick, the vice president of Focus on the Family, a Colorado-based conservative group.
>
> "The world of politics has eroded and encroached on areas that in previous generations were the rights of parents," he said. "People are protecting traditional values in education because that battle is occurring near their doorstep." (Harp, 1994, p. 12)

Albert R. Hunt, in his column "Politics and People" in the *Wall Street Journal,* calls the Religious Right a GOP albatross. He sees the Religious Right as a thundercloud hovering over the bright Republican political hopes for the fall of 1994 and beyond. According to Hunt, Christian activists are dominating the party from South Carolina to Washington State, from Iowa to Texas. He notes that there is a real yearning for a moral, even spiritual, revival and cites the phenomenal success of Bill Bennett's *Book of Virtues.* What he expects will happen is that the obnoxious tactics of the Fundamentalist candidates nominated will hurt senatorial or gubernatorial prospects in Virginia, Texas, and Minnesota. Moreover, he sees a half dozen or more seats in the House that will remain in Democratic hands because of the distaste for Religious Right Republican nominees (Hunt, 1994, p. A15).

The Fundamentalists are angry with any notion that they are a problem. Indeed, Christian activists, like the shrewd Ralph Reed who runs Pat Robertson's Christian Coalition, claim that criticism of them amounts to religious bigotry.

Cal Thomas (1994), the conservative columnist for the Los Angeles Times Syndicate, illustrates the backlash from criticism of the Religious Right in a column entitled " 'Religious Right' vs. 'Pagan Left.' " He chastises his fellow pundits for the harsh language they used describing the primary nomination of Oliver North for United States senator in Virginia. Frank Rich *(New York Times)* said the "radical right" is dangerous even when it loses. Susan Estrich accused "religious extremists" of coming out of the closet and beating the system. Thomas insists "that used to be called democracy before what ought to be called the Pagan Left decided that only people who think as they do are entitled to hold office." Thomas charges John Judis with class snobbery by referring to conservative Christians as "Wal-Mart Republicans."

The conservative thesis is that "something has gone dreadfully wrong in America. We have won the cold war but we have lost the culture war." Now, the conservatives argue that more people fear drugs and guns in school than they do someone who might say a prayer over the public address system.

> The Pagan Left smears conservative Christians by conjuring up images of snake handlers because it has lost on the issues. It raises the specter of imposed morality but can't defend its imposed immorality which has produced, according to the Census Bureau, the highest divorce rate in the nation, the highest teen pregnancy rate, the most abortions, the highest percentage of children raised in single-parent homes, the highest percentage of violent deaths among the young, and a male homicide rate that is four times higher than any other developed country except Mexico. (Thomas, 1994, p. B11)

Thomas insists that Americans want the moral underpinnings of the nation repaired. The government and politicians can't do all of the rebuilding, but they can be kept from further eroding the foundation. That's what this fall's election is about, and that will be the central issue for the White House in the next two years.

COALITION TO FIGHT BACK

When this series of essays (later to be department columns in *International Journal of Educational Reform*) was being prepared during the summer of 1992, public school administrators and their counterparts in teachers' unions, women's organizations, and main-line churches were ill-prepared to deal with the Religious Right's assault on public education. Two years later, the same groups were forming ad hoc alliances to cope with the real threat to schools. Where tame language was used in 1993, blunt warnings were being issued in June of 1994.

- "Religious extremists who are well-organized, highly disciplined, politically savvy, and deeply committed pose grave threats to American freedoms and institutions."
- "Clothed in righteous morality, they use religion as an ideological shield for a mean-spirited agenda."
- "The political movement often called the 'Religious Right' is rigid and narrow; it allows for no gray areas and clearly assigns an inferior role to women."

These are comments made by panelists at a Des Moines, Iowa, symposium entitled *Unmasking Religious Extremism in Iowa*. The panel consisted of the President of the Iowa Chapter of the National Organization for Women, the Associate Director of the Iowa State Education Association, and the Executive Director of the Des Moines Area Religious Council.

According to the panel, several conclusions can be drawn regarding the agenda of the Fundamentalists and their leaders:

1. The religious extremists in the political arena have charismatic leaders who are absolutely certain that they know what the problems and solutions are. There is no room for dialogue and compromise. Their attitude is confrontational. They have all of the answers.
2. The widespread feeling that things are out of control in society fuels the popularity of the extremist groups. They offer answers to all the frustration. Their answer is that to return to biblical principles, uniformly enforced, can save our society.
3. Increasingly, there is a free floating anxiety about ourselves as a culture. We have turned in upon ourselves. We, as a culture, are adrift.

Anxiety about sexuality, about our children and their education, and about our society as a whole have helped produce the Religious Right's agenda.

SHOULD FUNDAMENTALISTS OPT OUT?

Increasingly, public school leaders are saying maybe we ought to let them go, maybe we ought to let these people and their children opt out. When public schools won't make any accommodation, Fundamentalists are driven out of the public schools to independent schools or to home schooling.

Historically, the "opt out" solution has not been palatable to the vast majority of Americans who support public schools. James Conant, while president of one of our premier private universities in the 1950s, used to argue that the greater the proportion of United States youth who fail to attend our public schools and who receive their education elsewhere, the greater the threat to our democratic unity. Present-day opponents of the voucher system have successfully used the argument that allowing each subculture to start its own schools will only foster more divisiveness.

James Moffet, a reading expert who has developed several successful reading programs, argues that "America needs to accommodate plurality within unity, so that various parties can pursue, on the same sites, the ramifications of their goals and values and discover where these lead."

Whether we believe America's metaphor is a melting pot, a stir fry, or a tossed salad, the public school is the logical place to build the foundation of a peaceful, pluralistic society. It follows, then, that we should do what we can to keep Fundamentalists (and other religious dissidents) in the public schools. Just as we excuse students from certain health education sessions (or the entire course), we should be willing to allow students to skip an occasional book, class, or assignment.

Fundamentalist youths benefit from attending a public school, and their presence contributes to the democratic mission of public education. In school they acquire information and attitudes they wouldn't otherwise get. Steven Bates (1993) notes that a current study of textbooks used in Fundamentalist schools concluded that such books create a "permanent ghetto of the minds." Bates makes a strong case for keeping Fundamentalists in public schools saying, "We shouldn't panic when the difference manifests itself, as when some students leave the room or read a different book. Embracing diversity but forbidding its public expression is a crabbed form of pluralism."

WHAT WILL HAPPEN TO THE PUBLIC SCHOOLS?

The United States public schools have survived continuous attacks by friends and foes since the end of World War II. They need to improve, most everyone agrees. Unfortunately, they are easier to ignore, or freeze in time, than they are to significantly change. The labels change from "school improvement" to "school reform" to "school restructuring." Still, achievement seems to stay at the same level or decline, according to which set of statistics you trust.

School teachers, administrators, and board members will need allies, strategies, and considerable knowledge of the Fundamentalist opposition to stem the tide of negativism that is sweeping the country. The Clinton administration believes that Goals 2000: Educate America is the way to go. Fundamentalists want vouchers as a quick solution for their children and "competition" to solve the long-term problem of schools that don't educate and students that don't learn. In the next three chapters, the alternatives will be closely examined, and in the final chapter, I will pull together what has been learned about survival and victory in the school culture wars.

The fighting should become even more vicious as both the Fundamentalists and public schools attempt to make Goals 2000 fail or succeed. John Broder who writes for the Los Angeles Times/Washington Post Service puts it best, "This is less a contest between strong adversaries with some mutual respect than a holy war filled by bitterness and personal loathing."

ENDNOTES

1. Pat Robertson's use of the term ACLJ is a deliberate play on the American Civil Liberties Union abbreviation ACLU.
2. *Educational Leadership* and the *Kappan* have been most interested in OBE.

Towers, writing in the *Kappan,* reported that positive results were claimed by the Department of Education in Minnesota regarding increased student self-esteem, improved attendance, higher achievement of learner outcomes, better grades, higher SAT scores, and increased teacher/student satisfaction with school. ASCD's *Educational Leadership* support for OBE included: Alan S. Brown, "Outcome-Based Education: A Success Story," *Educational Leadership,* October 1988, p. 12; A. David Briggs, "Alhambra High: A 'High Success' School," *Educational Leadership,* October 1988, pp. 10–11; Charles E. Sambs, "One District Learns about Restructuring," *Educational Leadership,* April 1990, pp. 72–75; and Maureen Buffington, "Organizing for Results in High School English," *Educational Leadership,* October 1988, pp. 9–10.

REFERENCES

Americans United. 1993. *Madalyn Murray O'Hair and Ten Other Myths about Church and State.* Silver Spring, MD: Americans United for Separation of Church and State.

Associate News. 1994. "Associates Characterize Influence of Fundamentalist Christian Groups," *Association for Supervision and Curriculum Development* (Spring):1–2.

Balajthy, E. 1987. "The Tennessee Judicial Decision on Religion and Reading Basal Series: An Update and Implications for Reading Educators," Report No. CS 008 913, Baltimore, MD: Annual Meeting of the College Reading Association (ERIC Document Reproduction Service No. ED 285 141).

Balajthy, E. 1988. "Confrontation and Alienation: Education's Flawed Response to Religious Textbook Objections," Report No. CS 009 249, Atlanta, GA: Annual Meeting of the College Reading Association (ERIC Document Reproduction Service No. ED 297.

Bates, S. 1993. *Battleground: One Mother's Crusade, the Religious Right, and the Struggle for the Control of Our Classrooms.* New York: Poseidon Press.

Bazyn, B. 1994. "Who Is Harassed – Professor or Students?" *The Des Moines Register* (March 29):9A.

Binnie, I. 1994. "America's Religious Wars," *The Des Moines Register* (February 9):9A.

Bloom, A. 1987. *The Closing of the American Mind.* New York: Simon and Schuster.

Bloom, B. 1974. "An Introduction to Mastery Learning Theory," in *Schools, Society, and Mastery Learning,* J. H. Block (Ed.), New York: Holt, Rinehart and Winston, pp. 4–14.

Bloom, B. 1976. *Human Characteristics and School Learning.* New York: McGraw-Hill.

Bloom, B. 1981. *All Our Children Learning.* New York: McGraw-Hill.

Boston, R. 1994. "Public Schools under Seige," *Church and State,* 47(4):4–9, 20.

Brandt, R. 1992. "On Outcome-Based Education: A Conversation with Bill Spady," *Educational Leadership* (Dec.):66–70.

Brandt, S. (Ed.). 1994. "The Challenge of Outcome-Based Education," *Educational Leadership*, 51(6).

Carroll, J. 1963. "A Model for School Learning," *Teachers College Record*, 64:723–733.

Clarke, T. E. 1988. "Spirituality, Justice, and Cultural Evangelization," *Religion Education*, 83(1):53–66.

Cotherman, A. M. 1994. "OBE Scaring Us away from Real Issues," *Casper Star-Tribune* (Feb.):A4.

Darin, J. 1994. "A Return to Basics Is Best Answer for Gwinnett Classes," *Atlanta Journal* (Feb. 13):G2.

Dorrien, G. 1993. *The Neoconservative Mind: Politics, Culture, and the War of Ideology*. Philadelphia: Temple University Press.

Economist. 1994. "Classless Society: At-Home Schools," *The Arizona Republic* (June 15):B9.

Engel v. Vitale. 1962. 370 U.S. 421.

English, F. W. and P. A. Zirkel. 1990. "The Great Monkey Trial: *Scopes* in Perspective," *National Forum of Applied Educational Research Journal*, 2(2):4–17.

Falwell, J. 1979. *America Can Be Saved*. Garden City, NY: Doubleday.

Finn, C. E., Jr. 1990. "The Biggest Reform of All," *Phi Delta Kappan* (April):583–587.

1993. "Freedom of Thought and Public Education," *American Association of School Administrators* (Dec.):1, 3, 5, 7.

Fulbright, L. 1994. "OBE Retains Wide Support Despite Recent Setbacks," *Leadership News* (March 15):1–3.

Guskey, T. R. 1985. *Implementing Mastery Learning*. Belmont, CA: Wadsworth, p. xiii.

Harp, L. 1994. "A G.O.P. Divided Drives Wedge in Party," *Education Week* (June):12.

Herman, J. J. and J. L. Herman. 1993. *People and Education: The Human Side of Schools*, Vol. 1. Newbury, CA: Corwin Press.

Hudson, K. 1993. *Reinventing America's Schools: A Practical Guide to Components of Restructuring and Non-Traditional Education*, Vol. 3. Costa Mesa, CA: NACE/CEE, Box 3200, 92628.

Hunt, A. R. 1994. "The Religious Right Is a G.O.P. Albatross," *The Wall Street Journal* (June 9):A15.

Hunter, M. 1985. "What's Wrong with Madeline Hunter?" *Educational Leadership*, 42:57–60.

Hutchings, N. W. 1994. "Is Outcome-Based Education against the Law," *The Prophetic Observer*, Southwest Radio Church, P. O. Box 1144, Oklahoma City, OK.

1991. "Introduction to Education That Is Outcome Based," one-page handout, Minnesota State Department of Education, St. Paul.

Keller, F. 1968. "Goodbye, Teacher," *Journal of Applied Behavior Analysis,* 1:79–89.
Knicker, C. R. (Ed.). 1985a. *Religion and Public Education,* Vol. 12. Ames, IA: National Council on Religion and Public Education.
Knicker, C. R. (Ed.). 1985b. *Teaching about Religion in the Public Schools.* Bloomington, IN: Phi Delta Kappa Educational Foundation.
Kniker, C. R. (Ed.). 1991. *Religion and Public Education,* Vol. 18. Ames, IA: National Council on Religion and Public Education.
Lawton, M. 1994. "Girls Will- and Should-Be Girls," *Education Week* (March 30):24, 25, 26, 27.
Leslie, S. 1994. "Finding Common Ground: A New Strategy," *Free World Research Report* (Feb.):1, 6, 7.
Licklider, B. L. and C. R. Kniker. 1993. "Religious Issues Present Challenges to School Principals," *Religion and Public Education,* 20(1–3):106–112.
Lohman, D. F. 1993. "Learning and the Nature of Educational Measurement," *NASSP Bulletin* (Oct.):41–53.
Manatt, R. P. 1994. "Seeking a Middle Ground for School Reform–Meeting the Challenge of the Conservatives and Evangelicals," *International Journal of Educational Reform,* 3(2):226–241.
Manning, A. 1994a. "Curriculum Battles from Left and Right," *USA Today* (March 3):5D.
Manning, A. 1994b. "Focus on Outcome Starts an Uproar," *USA Today* (March 3):5D.
McGuire, D. 1994. "Most Callers Oppose Outcome-Based Education," *The Kansas City Star* (March 8):A-3.
Minnesota Department of Education. 1991. *Introduction to Education That Is Outcome-Based.* St. Paul: State of Minnesota Printing Office.
Mozart v. Hawkins County Public Schools (E.D. Tenn. 1985). 647 F. Supp. 1194, rev'd. 827 F.2d 1058 (6th Cir 1987).
Power, F. C. and K. D. Lapsley. (Eds.). 1992. *The Challenge of Pluralism Education, Politics, and Values.* Notre Dame: University of Notre Dame Press.
Quimby, D. 1994. "Tips for Principals," *National Association of Secondary School Principals* (April):1–2.
1993. "The Religious Right: Beliefs, Goals and Strategies," *Horace Mann League Board of Directors,* p. 1A.
Ritter, J. 1994. "Growing Push for School Prayer," *USA Today* (March 18):3A.
Schweitzer, A. 1956. *The Quest of the Historical Jesus.* New York: MacMillan.
Scopes v. State (Tenn. 1927). 289 S. W. 363.
Simbro, W. 1994. "Fight 'Extremism' Panel Urges," *Des Moines Register* (June 13):7A.
Simonds, R. L. 1993a. *A Guide to the Public Schools.* Costa Mesa, CA: NACE/CEE, Box 3200, 92628.
Simonds, R. L. 1993b. *Presence Report.* Costa Mesa, CA: National Association of Christians/Educators/Citizens for Excellence and Education, p. 3.

Spady, W. G. 1988. "Organizing for Results: The Basis of Authentic Restructuring and Reform," *Educational Leadership,* 46(2):4–8

Spady, W. G. 1992. "It's Time to Take a Close Look at Outcome-Based Education," *Outcomes* (Summer):6–13.

Thomas, C. 1994. " 'Religious Right' vs. 'Pagan Left,' " *The Arizona Republic* (June 17):B11.

Towers, J. M. 1994. "The Perils of Outcome-Based Teacher Education," *Phi Delta Kappan,* 75(8):624–627.

White, S. 1994. "Boysen Offers Concessions to Ministers on KERA," *Lexington Herald Leader* (March 3):A1, A6.

Whitehead, J. W. 1994. "With Free Help, the Religious Turn Litigious," *The Wall Street Journal* (Feb. 17):B1, B12.

CHAPTER 2

The Attack on "Government Schools" Blunts School Reform

WOW, have we got a fight on our hands! The Religious Right was supposed to go away with George Bush. He kept the faith with cultural conservatives; he even turned over his nomination convention to them, but only the *evangelical* Protestants stuck with him on election day. Now, school reform could move quickly to Outcome-Based Education; standards for students; multicultural, nonsexist curricula; pluralism; long-range planning; and carefully selected language that wouldn't be offensive to any group. Rush Limbaugh and all of the Rush wannabes in each media market would soon be silent.

The Right didn't go away. The liberal lobbying group, People for the American Way, estimates that the Religious Right made significant inroads in November, winning "hundreds, if not thousands, of seats in school boards, city councils, water districts and the like" (Mydans, 1993). In 500 races monitored by People for the American Way, Fundamentalist Christian candidates won about 40 percent of them because of Religious Right involvement. Members of Pat Robertson's Christian Coalition continue to make inroads in state Republican parties in Oregon, Iowa, and elsewhere. At present, they can't have their way on their agenda for choice and vouchers, but they can stop things from happening.

New York City won't have its Rainbow Curriculum, a gay contingent in the St. Patrick's Day Parade, or even its liberal school superintendent. *Heather Has Two Mommies* won't be a basic reference work for those planning the revised New York City curriculum. Even President Clinton found that he couldn't open the military to those openly gay even with a presidential decree. Each of these failed liberal power plays has given ammunition to conservatives nationwide.

An essay for *Time* magazine by Richard Brookhiser explains what happened.

> These seeming turnabouts are not examples of the people changing their mind. Rather, they are part of a process of people discovering their own mind, in response to the perceived power plays of minorities. Just because Americans didn't like the rhetoric of some of the conservatives at the Republican Convention doesn't mean they have liked the behavior of the liberals since. Each group stands convicted of the sin of bellicosity: the right for declaring (in Patrick Buchanan's words) a cultural war, the left for waging one. (Brookhiser, 1993)

On the surface, this appears to be a Hobbesian war fought between atheists and people who believe in God, by the thought police of the politically correct who denounce and try to silence those with whom they disagree, between the liberals and the conservatives. Civility, tolerance, and pluralism seem to have left this country, as they have Yugoslavia.

Education has a pretty good grasp of the need for reform for pre-K through graduate school—but most of our fellow citizens don't. We use language that goes over the heads of our families, friends, and school supporters. We speak in a jargon that is only understood by others in the "Fraternity." If you don't believe me, try "OBE," "America 2000," and "At-Risk children" on your barber or hairdresser. At the same time, educators, and the professors who prepare them, don't understand or even recognize the language of the Religious Right.

This book is directed toward those who prepare teachers, consultants, and administrators. Thus, the major thrust of this chapter will be toward developing an understanding of the conservative position(s). Nonetheless, a set of definitions of the educational reform movement and a superintendent's practical advice will be provided to help all sides of the struggle.

WHAT'S WRONG?

Pretend for a few minutes that you are listening to a call-in show during prime "drive time" [1]. Someone who looks like Larry King without his colorful braces starts the show with an editorial.

" 'If we open a quarrel between the past and the present, we shall find that we have lost the future.' Winston Churchill was speaking of postwar, United Kingdom politics, but today he could be describing the recent battle between the educational leadership and the religious right over modernizing the public school curriculum.

"Alarmed by the growing number of high school graduates who can't cope with life in the real world, state and local educational leaders are shifting the focus from how much time is spent in the classroom to what graduates actually know. The methodology for this shift in emphasis is called Outcome-Based Education, the brainchild of educational consultant William Spady, which sets specific achievement levels students must reach in each subject before graduation.

"The Religious Right, on the other hand, believes that public schools could, by returning to the biblically based beliefs of the 1950s, lead the United States once again to a position of respect and power in the world.

"It's the position of this radio station and this commentator that America's schools are in deep trouble. Frankly, we don't know much about restructuring or outcomes, but we know something must be done. What do you, the listeners, think? We go to line three. . . ."

The first few calls are from students.

"In my school the teachers are all afraid of the administration. They stifle creativity. Kids just want to know what the right answers are for the tests!"

"We spend millions of dollars in my community for school buildings, but we pay teachers peanuts."

"I'm a college student. I would like to teach, but I would need more money than a starting teacher makes!"

"One big difference that I see in the United States' school system and other countries is that we don't have any national expectations. How will we ever compete if there are no national requirements?"

"We have no tracking so all of the kids are mixed together.

Thus, the teacher has to go down to the lowest learning level and that bores the brighter kids and you lose them."

Next, after the ubiquitous station break and a commercial selling "micro-thickening" for balding men, a number of adults call. The first, apparently very concerned about declining achievement, says, "What has happened in education is that the educational bureaucracy spends too much time and attention on how to teach with little attention to what is taught." He goes on to say, "The teachers who really knew their subjects are retiring—now we're left with teachers who are not well educated!"

In rapid sequence, you listen to several callers who are talking about public schools in a manner that seems almost like gibberish to you.

"The state-controlled 'government schools' are based on tyranny. It inevitably breeds widespread failure. The American people have been fighting the evils of communism everywhere but in their own land."

"Eliminating the public schools will open a vast market which will be quickly filled by moral, successful, competing private schools."

"I just had to take a course in human relations to get a teacher's license in this state. The course was filled with New Age philosophy, you know that stuff that the Carnegie Foundation, the Rockefellers, and Ted Turner are pushing. I knew right away. I saw through it because they tried to get me to meditate and they had activities that were blatantly labeled 'values clarification,' 'humanism,' and 'Outcome-Based Education.'"

"Do your listeners know that the Parents as Teachers (PAT) Program will put a state-designated 'parent educator' in your home a minimum of eight times a year to monitor whether you are a good parent? This will result in state control of children and reduce parents to the status of breeders and supervised custodians. They have these twelve categories of at-risk kids and every family in America could fit into one of these categories!"

Finally, a school teacher gets the line. "You folks have talked about how bad it is in our schools and keep suggesting that all we have to do is go back to the way we did things in the 1950s. Look at how different it is for kids and teachers today. The American family is getting weaker, fewer families go to church, and kids grow up so much faster. I just read in *Time* that 55 percent of our high school kids have had intercourse by the time they are seventeen. Besides, we have children of vastly different backgrounds. We can't just teach the basics anymore."

The more you listen, the harder it is to separate fact from fiction, and to distinguish constructive change from conspiracy. Imagine how difficult it is for a parent, a board member, or a taxpayer who has no understanding of the many federal and state programs supporting research, restructuring, transforming, or even categorical aid. Then, too, everyone has become so nasty. Some educators and their professional organizations automatically reject anyone who questions where the schools are going as secret agenda–carrying right-wingers. That's simply not true. Parents and patrons really do need to know what replaced phonics. Business leaders understandably want workers who make good products and who make the customers happy. To denounce them is to divert attention away from the much needed struggle to improve schools.

"Other circles allege a dark statist conspiracy to dumb down the populace so it will automatically obey government's dictates. That's absurd, too" (Flansburg, 1993).

THE ROOTS OF THE RELIGIOUS RIGHT

The battle has been brewing since the early 1980s. The Moral Majority, led by Fundamentalist preacher Jerry Falwell, vowed to bring "atheist" public education to an end. The plan was to replace it with a free enterprise, Christian school system. Falwell, Pat Robertson, Mel and Norma Gabler (the textbook censors from Longview, Texas), and Phyllis Schlafly, to name but a few, objected to no prayers in school and secular humanism, which they contended was the "religion" of the public schools that teachers were indoctrinating in the nation's children. They defined humanism as the belief that "man" is in control of his own destiny instead of being put on earth to carry out a divine plan.

Secular humanism, school prayer, vouchers to pay for private school tuition, and tax limitations all became symbols for the movement that was soon named the "New Right." Members of the New Right worked hard to elect Ronald Reagan, but his two terms did little to advance their agenda. When Bush was defeated in 1992, many thought the movement was dead—or at least close to it.

While the New Right was reorganizing and doing some interesting "research" and publications, educators nationwide became convinced that *A Nation at Risk* and its related reports calling for reform were more than just teacher bashing. Public schools were not getting the job done!

EDUCATORS' LOOSE LANGUAGE

A consensus developed that educators in the United States did need to change. We were behind other postindustrial nations in achievement, and we were not serving the needs of our very diverse student population. Concomitant with the worldwide movement toward decentralization, teachers, administrators, and school board members realized that top-down reform wouldn't work. Educators could and should control the change process.

Federal, state, and local initiatives followed. Many were clearly research-based; others were simply based on common sense. To seasoned educators, it all made sense: school transformation, Outcome-Based Education, vertical leadership teams, school-based management, global education, drug education programs, whole language (as an approach to reading), cooperative learning, America 2000, and higher order thinking skills. Indeed, each of these efforts at educational reform had been well researched and made good sense for *public* schools. Criterion-referenced testing and authentic assessment would be used at local, state, and national levels to prove reform's success.

Unfortunately, educators have an in-group language that the general public doesn't understand and that often provides a host of red flags for those who are looking for them (Iowa State Education Association, 1993). What educators and politicians meant when they talked about education reform and cutting edge research was not what Religious Right followers heard. Table 2.1 helps you to listen with the red flag filter on.

Table 2.1. Education terms redefined by the Religious Right.

The Religious Right's Definition	The Real Definition
Critical Thinking: Learning to criticize your parents, question values.	*Critical Thinking:* Higher order thinking skills to make sound decisions: synthesis, analysis, evaluation.
Cooperative Learning: One dumb kid learning from another dumb kid.	*Cooperative Learning:* Students working in groups of three or four to do team problem solving. The teacher carefully blends the group composition for maximum learning growth of all participants.
Global Education: Promotes vegetarianism and attempts to eliminate patriotism by telling children that our country isn't the best.	*Global Education:* The study of cultures, economics, languages, governments and ecosystems worldwide.
Government Schools: The neighborhood school captured by the secular humanists.	*Government Schools:* Public School.
Humanism: The religion the public school teachers are indoctrinating in the nation's children; "Man above God."	*Humanism:* The study of human beings, their achievements and interests rather than of abstract beings and problems of theology.
New Age Religion: A diabolical worldwide plot to replace Christianity with Satanism.	*New Age Religion:* A myth.
Outcome-Based Education: Indoctrination of politically correct values to replace religious and traditional values for the purpose of turning students into robots.	*Outcome-Based Education:* Curriculum/assessment approach that sets specific achievement levels, which students must reach in each subject before they graduate.
Politically Correct: Language that is deliberately misleading to brainwash. Nothing is sin!	*Politically Correct:* Language selected so as not to hurt others, e.g., "African American," not "Colored."
Quest Drug Education Program: Teaches children to say "no" to their parents; doesn't differentiate between right and wrong; teachers who are not licensed to practice psychiatry perform therapy on students (ditto most other programs aimed at helping students develop self-esteem or life skills).	*Quest Drug Education Program:* A carefully prepared, successful program sponsored by the Lion's Club nationwide. Helps youth stand up to peer pressure and say "no" to drugs.
School Transformation: A takeover by the teachers' unions and other humanists to promote the beliefs of New Age Religion rather than traditional and family values. Throws out the basic skills.	*School Transformation:* Changing the use of time, instructional methods, and the organization of the school to improve student achievement. Enhances the basic skills.

(continued)

Table 2.1. (continued).

The Religious Right's Definition	The Real Definition
Teacher-as-Coach: Teacher should be authority figure, not discussion group leader. What are we paying them for, anyway?	*Teacher-as-Coach:* The teacher facilitates learning by skillfully guiding the process. Less memorization, more active learning takes place.
Whole Language: Learning to look, see, guess—teaches reading without the "proven phonics method" and traditional grammatical usage and form.	*Whole Language:* An integrated approach to teaching language skills and reading. Uses literature anthologies rather than repetitive "Dick and Jane" stories.

In contrast, examine the clear language used by *U.S. News and World Report* ("The Perfect School," 1993) in describing an amalgam of the reforms being contemplated by educators and researchers. Describing the "Perfect School—Nine Reforms to Revolutionize American Education," the article included:

1. Teachers as entrepreneurs
2. Slashing the bureaucracy
3. Training in the classroom
4. Life-is-more curriculum
5. Testing student performance
6. Incentives for good teaching
7. Technology for learning
8. Choice and competition
9. Stretching the year

THE CHRISTIAN COALITION

Those who would understand what the "Christian Right," the "Religious Right," or simply "Fundamentalists" want must keep in mind that their common thread is not Christianity per se. Rather, it is that they see strict Christian ideology as the only cure for the moral decline in American society: a decline they are convinced is caused by the "humanistic" teachings of the public schools. Their rallying cry is "family values" (ISEA, 1993).

Depending on the part of the country you call home, a different Christian organization may appear to be the most influential in school politics: the Christian Coalition in Virginia Beach, Virginia; Citizens for Excellence in Education in Santa Ana, California; Focus on the Family in Colorado Springs, Colorado; and the Eagle Forum in Afton, Illinois, are the best known. The American Coalition for Traditional Values and Concerned Women for America are lesser powers.

Key to the war on public schools is Pat Robertson's Christian Coalition. Robertson is thought of as a "Crossfire" panelist on CNN or as an unsuccessful presidential candidate—essentially, though, he is a television evangelist. The Christian Coalition encourages its members to get involved in local grass-roots politics. Unless they tip their hands by overreacting to school Halloween parties or demanding to see and keep all of the tests their children take [2], you don't know they are there because of deliberate "stealth" politics. They avoid public forums, preferring instead to surprise the conventional candidates by write-in campaigns at the last minute and by carefully orchestrated get-out-the-vote efforts that start with potluck dinners at Fundamentalist churches. School board hopefuls from this group will neglect to reveal any real agenda or Christian ties during their campaigns.

In private, Republican party regulars in Iowa will tell of their bewilderment over the state's Republican Party platform adopted last year. Mainstream Republicans were outworked, outfinanced and embarrassed by the network of state and national organizations under the banner of the Christian Right. First, they took over the caucuses. Then they took seven of the seventeen seats on the State Republican Central Committee, wrote the state platform, and held at least forty-six of the fifty seats at the 1992 GOP National Convention.

The platform they wrote is quite instructive. It wasn't just conservative; it was extremist. It called for abolishing the Federal Reserve Board and curtailing the United Nations. Regarding education, it advocated the dismissal of Iowa Department of Education

Director William Lepley and the dismantling of both the state and national education departments. It also asserted:

> We oppose the promotion of secular humanism, "political correctness," New Age concepts, the PETA [3] philosophy, one-world government, situational ethics, and the teaching of homosexuality as an acceptable lifestyle or behavior. We support repeal of Iowa's Global Education mandate, the Human Growth and Development mandate, and the America 2000 plan.

Why does the Christian Right want to take over the public schools by taking over school boards? Their publications are quite clear on their intent. The Christian Coalition has a number of allied groups dedicated to "taking over the public school system." None is more strident or influential than Citizens for Excellence in Education (CEE), based in Santa Ana and headed by Robert Simonds. Two publications, *Educating for the New World Order* (1990) by B. K. Eakman and *A Critique of America 2000: An Education Strategy* (1991) by K. Simonds, explain the Christian Right's reason for targeting schools.

According to the doctrine espoused by Simonds, Eakman, and their followers, parents have given permission to the school to *teach academic subjects only*. In their view, the family and the church are responsible for all other aspects of children's lives. Rather than "public schools," they use the term *government* schools, insisting that what we have now are agencies for indoctrination of docile followers.

They see curricula to provide for children from diverse backgrounds (such as the Rainbow Curriculum adopted by some subdistricts in New York City) as "pro-homosexual," promoting "New Age Religion" (an advanced stage of secular humanism), and persecuting Christians. Efforts by public schools to restructure or transform, and interest in the "whole child" infringes on the family by introducing ideas and values inconsistent with those of the family and church.

The Citizens for Excellence in Education (with either Robert or Kathi Simonds as spokesperson) believe that a great spiritual battle is in progress. In this battle, one side believes that parents must "take back" the public schools. On the other side (according to the Simonds) is the left-wing education establishment, which includes the National Education Association, the American Civil Liberties Union, and People for the American Way. Robert Simonds wrote in 1985, in a booklet entitled "How to Elect Christians to Public Office":

> We need strong school board members who know right from wrong. The Bible being the only true source on right and wrong, should be the guide of board members. Only Godly Christians truly qualify for this important position. . . . ("Religious Right Targets Education," 1993; ISEA, 1993; Simonds, 1991)

HOW CAN THE RELIGIOUS RIGHT BELIEVE THESE THINGS?

Many theological scholars have studied the impact of the baby boomers who dropped out of organized religion as they grew up. In the 1960s, their parents made them go to the church or synagogue. Estimates of youthful church experience run as high as 95 percent for the boomers, but most dropped out as they became adults. Forty-two percent still are dropouts ("The Generation That Forgot God," 1993), but huge numbers have returned, and not to mainline Protestantism and Judaism.

When they return, the boomer wants a stronger message than that offered by the affluent, predominately white, liberal denominations that date from colonial times. Now these churches are on the defensive, losing members and influence. Meanwhile, churches on the two spiritual extremes are growing fast: conservative evangelical Protestantism on one pole, and an assortment of Eastern New Age and unconventional religions on the other. Analysts say mainliners are suffering because they have failed to transmit a compelling Christian message to their own children or to anyone else ("The Generation That Forgot God," 1993, p. 47).

The two extremes, conservative evangelical Protestantism and Eastern New Age and unconventional religion, have swelling ranks filled with people in their twenties to forties who haven't had much contact with religion in the past two decades. Both extremes are suspicious of the other. Both extremes think that what they have discovered spiritually will also be best for their children.

Public school educators, for the most part, have not gone through this dropping out and rediscovery. Many have stayed with the old line Protestant Churches or the Catholic Church. A large number of public school teachers, similar to their age peers, are what theological statisticians call "believers but not belongers."

ATTENDING A RELIGIOUS RIGHT SEMINAR

An offhand comment by one of our student assistants at the School Improvement Model Office at Iowa State University led to my first contact with the Religious Right as an observer. (I had met them plenty of times when I was the speaker working with schools and parents for improvement in student achievement.)

My undergraduate friend and coworker said, "Did you know we are entering the Age of Aquarius and are leaving the Age of Pisces?"

I retorted, "I thought that happened in 1968?"

My friend said, "In my church we have been studying what this change means and what it's doing to our schools. The New Age Movement is the Age of Aquarius and it's based on humanism and pantheism."

"I have a pretty good idea of what you mean by *humanism* but I don't understand *pantheism*," I replied.

He didn't either, but he said that an expert on the New Age Movement's harm to public schools was speaking at his church that very night—would I like to attend?

A bit surprised at the early starting time (6:30 P.M.) for a lecture, I came to his church on a cold, frosty night. The church was a new building, large, and one I knew to have a very rapidly growing Fundamentalist congregation located not far from our campus. Five dollars for the offering and four dollars for the forty-seven–page seminar handbook got me into the sanctuary.

Brannon Howse was the speaker, and the introduction to the seminar manual identifies him as a resident of St. Paul, Minnesota, married but with no children. "Brannon desires to challenge, encourage, and assist Christians in living victorious Christian lives, through his sermon and concert ministry as well as through his writings." Apparently, his ministry involves a summer series of Sunday night outdoor hymn sings in St. Paul's Como Park.

The seminar handbook was entitled *The New Age Is Not So New*. Divided into three parts—(1) The New Age, and Introduction; (2) The Six Main Beliefs of the New Age; and (3) The Doctrines of the New Age—the handbook at first appeared to be a type of programmed learning. As he began his lecture, I realized that the numbered blanks sprinkled throughout the pages were meant to be filled in with the answers he provided on 35 mm slides. Giving the booklet a quick perusal, I could find nothing about education or public schools except for an attack on Jill Anderson's Pumsey Program. He included a letter to parents for Unit I of Pumsey and explains that the program is used to teach positive thinking skills. "Notice the subtle, humanistic, New Age theme," Howse writes. "The emphasis on rejecting anything that makes the child feel 'bad' about herself assures that he or she would never admit to being a sinner in need of a Savior" (Howse, 1991, p. 18).

After looking over the crowd of some 500 men and women, mostly ages twenty to thirty-five and all of whom seemed to have purchased the manual, I stole a quick look at the "six main beliefs of the New Age." Although instructed by a slide on the screen not to get ahead of the presentation, it was lucky that I took a brief peek—we never returned to the booklet once Mr. Howse began!

The six main beliefs were

1. A new world is coming.
2. All is one.
3. God is everything and everything is God.
4. We are all God.
5. We must tap into our collective unconscious (altered states).
6. All religions are one.

Out of these beliefs of the New Age, Howse builds a conspiracy of a growing occult known as the New Age Movement. The book jacket blurb assures the reader that "the seminar will reveal what every Christian should know about this subtle and deceptive counterfeit and how it is effecting the traditional Judeo-Christian family." A testimonial on the back cover by Robert G. Morrison declares, "To improve education, what we really need is parental choice. Brannon Howse helps parents assert their rights and defend their children."

Mr. Howse began to speak. He was slightly built and of medium height. He looked to be about thirty years old. Although he held the remote control for his carousel projector, he seldom used the slides. In front of the stage were two folding banquet tables covered with books, pamphlets, and handwritten notes stapled in batches of forty to fifty pages each. His presentation was rapid fire, disjointed, and quite emotional. He repeatedly picked up various publications on the table with the comment, "I have all that documented here!" Promising a question and answer period after we took a mid-evening break, he spoke for three hours without a break.

He started by saying he would talk a lot about public schools. Referring to current events, he said, "If Congress can't run a two-bit bank and a two-bit post office, it has no business running schools!" Howse, in a rambling discourse, moved from Parents as Teachers, to Outcome-Based Education, Total Quality Management, situational ethics, the United Nations, home schooling, Transactional Analysis, world government, the Federal Reserve Bank, and America 2000:

> Let's look at what they are doing! Parents as Teachers—Laura Rogers was active in exposing this. The idea was that parents would be able to do more at home with their children. However, they forced children to take Ritalin. If you don't give it to your hyperactive kid they will fine you $1000.00 or put you in jail. They said, "Give your child the drug or we will remove your child." They have all kinds of codes they use to label your child at risk. Who's who to know what's what? They suggest that if the child has slow growth, if the parent is unable to cope—that parent as a teacher program is a smoke screen for *teachers* as parents.

> Now let's talk about Outcome-Based Education. OBE was invented by Bill Spady and William Glaser. [He also reminded us that Ted Sizer has something to do with it.] OBE is OK if it centers on cognitive knowledge. But, 80 percent of what educators teach children in school is noncognitive knowledge. They are getting into attitudes, values, and emotions. If the child doesn't exhibit the correct response, they could be put back in classes and

get retraining. The dangerous thing about Outcome-Based Education is the control by state departments of education, not by legislators.

We now have this thing called Total Quality Management, TQM. TQM says to you, "Guys, here are the specs." It is just like at an airplane plant. You can have good morale but they still have to build a Cessna. TQM is simply a way to implement OBE. In this seminar tonight we are exposing Satan's lies. Satan is really fighting us on this seminar. The New Age is

1. Occult (Satanic things) and metaphysics
2. Superstition
3. New Age asks you to find yourself as a means of salvation instead of having God find you.

You're supposed to find God within yourself. They stress unlimited human potential. Man is God. Use the power of your mind. If you can conceive it, you can achieve it. Man is co-creator of the universe. The New Age is strong for a new world order. The New Age Movement is a self-made religion, government, and economics. The New Age Movement is the Apostasy, the period just before the last day. *Apostasy* is abandonment of one's religious faith. We are in a cycle, leaving the Age of Pisces and entering the Age of Aquarius. That is to extend up to the year 2001.

New Age people believe in Crystals which capture the healing ability. They also talk of *Good Karma* and the number 666 which sends out a message to outer space: "Come and Enter the New Age."

They pick up things from many other religions. For example, reincarnation, Good Karma or Higher State (I have dyslexia – I must have things concrete). Let me pose a question. If there is no right or wrong, how can you decide on reincarnation? How can they determine Good Karma? You can have your own "master guide."

What will give you the best outcome for yourself? Situation ethics. Christ was the leader for the Age of Pisces. Now man or the antichrist will lead in Aquarius. In the former age, one would say "I am a sinner and I need a savior." In the Age of Aquarius, we will have one world leader – that comes from the world government. Many people worry about the economic common market in Europe. The Bible says that ten kings will give up all their power to the New World Order. When the antichrist comes, they will give him all power. They will do that at the United Nations. New Age religion is real and it is a serious threat to us and our families. We can be judgmental. We must be harsh – can't always have a positive approach – think positive – but we must examine everyday what's happening.

We must remember the traditional family's quest for survival. We don't need bossy schools. They judge us. We want to teach the child. I am not telling you to pull the kids out of public schools and put them in a private school or home schools. I am telling you:

1. I am very disappointed in the public schools.
2. Why sacrifice your child? What would happen if you don't care?
3. For the right child, public schools are O.K.

Much [is] to be said for home schooling, however. This is the most important parenting decision you will ever make.

What are the problems with the public schools? First, Mass Indoctrination. Second, they are breeding ground for liberalism. Liberals are against the voucher system. We are paying $4500.00 for school. Why not spend $1500.00 for home schooling and save the rest for college? We have some fine public school teachers, but it is not a pretty picture. These are the facts. The Aquarius conspirators are in education. They want "power for [the] education system." We have great powers at school board. Christians need to run for school boards. Help someone run. The religion of humanism oozes from the public schools. If my religion is not allowed, why should theirs be? They have no rules. They use a cult technique: biofeedbacks, relaxation, guidelines, hugging, visualization, and consensus control of the mental processes. All this is illegal! [You've] got to be a licensed psychologist to do this. [He says OBE is behaviorist—teachers will not be responsible for giving children the "right" answers.] No F's, instead we will give them an "L" for "learning in progress!" What nonsense.

Values clarification [is] used in courses like Quest. Simon was quoted, "This is based on my work!" He then quotes Benedict who says, "Values clarification is very dangerous."

Howse lumps almost all programs to help youngsters deal with personal problems into the "can't do basket." He attacks Quest, DoSo, Pumsey—In Pursuit of Excellence, Project Charley and Impressions. Impressions (a K–6 reading series) is a favorite target of the Fundamentalists because it includes stories of fantasy and witches in its fairy tales, poems, and classic children's literature. "How could Harcourt, Brace and Jovanovich (HBJ) allow such a program for K–6 children when it includes cults, witchcraft and spends a whole month on Halloween?"

The HBJ publishing company has prepared a defense kit for

Impressions. This kit, which is comprised of testimonials from districts that have used Impressions successfully, has created a fanatic "war story" for the Christian Coalition. Apparently, Laura Rogers, in a protest before her school board, was able to grab a defense kit, take it under her arm and run. According to the folklore surrounding the incident, the school board was rude to her—now they treat her with respect.

Finally, Brannon Howse returned to Outcome-Based Education, and America 2000.

"We keep hearing," he said, "that OBE is needed to organize the learning over twelve years. It doesn't take twelve years to teach people. It takes twelve years to brainwash people!" He continued:

> Use Rush Limbaugh as a guide to how to handle these things. The NEA is for OBE.
>
> The NEA does not represent teachers; for example, teachers voted for Reagan. The NEA is financed by Rockefeller and Carnegie to get world government. California turned down their materials based on Marxism. The Rockefeller family donated land for the U.N. to promote globalism. Remember the Federal Reserve Bank is presided over by 300 stockholders. It is not an agency of the government. We have documentation that these guys are working toward globalism.
>
> We will see increased nationalization of our education. Education 2000 is an example. They got that through OBE; America 2000 is the federal government in charge of education. They have 12,000–14,000 employees in the Department of Education. They could operate with 900. To win, Bush was told he needed a program. Clinton and Senator Kennedy got involved. It's even smellier than it was. They have pulled choice out of there. They want to say [that] we want to nationalize education. The one-room school house was good enough. They talk about breaking the mold. America 2000 is so vague: everything the child needs, 6:00 A.M. to 6:00 P.M. [It] takes a whole community to raise a child, they say. What ever happened to the family being the center of the community? Schools will become the pivotal point. The six goals are for business. This will create employees who are overqualified. Then wages will go down.

Howse says that OBE gives mixed messages: don't have sex, but if you do, here's how to do it safely. He charges that political correctness is being taught instead of reading and writing; the rest is up to the parent. He ended with an attack on gay rights and having respect for gays:

> No first grader should be thinking about gay behavior; they should be thinking about recess and lunch. "Respect for all life styles and religions?" If you are gay, you will teach one side over the other. We've got it documented. No values. You can have Buddhist materials in the schools, but not the Bible. The day may come when we have to resist.

He goes back to talking about OBE: "Madeline Hunter invented mastery learning. Mastery learning is all right if cognitive skills are involved." Howse says he himself can't grasp abstract things:

> Under OBE, teachers will spend more and more on me. If you want everyone to slam dunk, you've got to lower the basket. *No*, discipline doesn't encourage creativity, it doesn't allow children to reach higher levels. It's mass indoctrination. I asked William Bennett, "What can I do? How can I help?" He said:
> 1. Pull your children out.
> 2. Work for choice.
> 3. Raise hell with the local school boards.
>
> Treat boards with respect. However, kill them with kindness. Do what Reagan did. The press hated what he stood for, but they couldn't help but like him; he was so smooth.

In all, Howse spoke from 6:30 to almost 10:00 P.M. without a break. He kept promising a question and answer period, but it never came. When he finally stopped, most of the audience headed for the restrooms or for the parking lot. When we came back, he was gone. I would have liked to ask about several erroneous statements that he made including:

- John Dewey wrote the *Communist Manifesto*.
- John Dewey had four of the Rockefeller brothers in his classes at Columbia and talked them into giving the land for the U.N. headquarters to promote globalism.
- Madeline Hunter invented Mastery Learning.

Obviously, Howse's grasp of the sweep of history and the facts would surprise Karl Marx, the Rockefellers (since Dewey only taught education courses and retired in 1930), and Ben Bloom and John Block, who certainly believe that they created mastery teaching for Mastery Learning. None of this made any difference to his audience, of course. Most were young parents or college students. As I watched them listen to Howse and thumb through the seminar manual, I saw no evidence of disbelief. On the contrary, I saw constant head nodding and heard groans each time the speaker made another claim that OBE promoted Satan, intruded upon a parent's rightful role, promoted values established by the government rather than the family, and diverted scarce resources and time away from academics.

A CHANGE IN TACTICS

Although Howse and his friend are still defending against Satanism and witchcraft, they are now tackling bigger projects. Multicultural programs that emphasize diversity and other cultures drive them up the wall (Jones, 1993). Any materials that contain information on homosexual lifestyles are certain targets. In New York City in May, for example, the Christian Coalition formed an unusual alliance with the Catholic Church that turned out a record number of voters to remove candidates who supported Chancellor Joseph A. Fernandez's multicultural curriculum (Dillon, 1993). Their rallying cry was the "Children of the Rainbow" curriculum, which includes information on gay and lesbian parents. Sex education, human development, and AIDS programs also are continually under fire (Jones, 1993).

Perhaps the most puzzling spectacle for mainline educators has been the nationwide attack on Outcome-Based Education. This struggle has centered, at first, on Pennsylvania's effort to overhaul its 159-year-old public education system. The Department of Education's plan would require students to master fifty-five academic "outcomes" or goals in ten subjects in order to graduate. The Citizens for Excellence in Education raised the usual objections. Parents were told that the plan would allow educators to teach New Age and occult beliefs and would force youngsters to learn about homosexuality. None of this is found in the regulations.

"Our critics are concerned that some influence other than their own will control their children's lives," says Joseph Bard, the state commissioner of elementary and secondary education. "They are reading too much into it or just telling falsehoods" ("Religious Right Targets Education," 1993, p. 9).

The CEE attack has been more sophisticated in the Pennsylvania battle. A 900 number was used to coordinate groups attending protests, a videocassette was produced, and State Rep. Ron Gamble (D-Allegheny), in opposition to the plan, published a monthly anti-OBE newsletter called the *Gamble-Gram*. By June of 1993, the Pennsylvania Department of Education and the governor had approved the plan, but the legislature was expected to stop it cold. To everyone's surprise, the legislature agreed with the governor, and OBE became a part of the state mandated curriculum, July 24, 1993.

Wyoming's Hot Springs County School District was confronted with a petition opposed to its OBE program. Kim Pippin, the protest spokesman, said that OBE was a national trend running contrary to family values, beliefs, and attitudes. He charged that OBE would assist students to fit into a "global, technological, culturally diverse society." OBE would involve taking too much time away from the three R's and would promote education based on attitudes and beliefs (Cloudwalker, 1993).

Oklahoma has provided an interesting face-off with Dr. William Spady, the father of OBE, on one side and Peg Luksik, an unsuccessful Pennsylvania gubernatorial candidate, on the other. Forty school districts in Oklahoma have been trying OBE under pilot projects set up by Spady, a sociologist from Eagle, Colorado. During a speaking tour of Oklahoma, Luksik, the author of a new book entitled *Who Controls the Children?*, a mother of six children and a former classroom teacher in Johnstown, Pennsylvania, says that any explanation of OBE's usefulness is nonsense. Luksik contends that there is a basic conflict between people who want to raise their own children and those who believe that the state should control the raising (Killackey, 1993).

Spady, who has had a distinguished career, including basic research with the Far West Laboratory at San Francisco and as an associate executive director of the American Association of School Administrators, once more found himself defending OBE and fighting against what he considers to be outrageous charges. He jokingly insisted that he's not the devil incarnate. Spady has visited Oklahoma several times to help public school districts using OBE during pilot projects. Spady insists that Outcome-Based Education is extremely elementary in concept. It's changing how we do business in schools. But it's just common sense. The OBE process establishes clearly defined goals and gives school children expanded opportunities to master those goals. Spady says that OBE doesn't eliminate A–F grading systems or traditional age-specific grades such as first, second, or third grade. OBE establishes a clarity of focus on outcomes of significance. OBE does stress re-testing, group learning, and "values" such as achievement, order, attendance, tolerance, diversity, citizenship, and respect.

OBE focuses more on what students need to learn in class–and focuses less on "seat time" in specific time blocks in traditional school days, semesters, and academic years. Moreover, Spady insists that he would never have approved of the 7000 organized learner outcomes that were considered in Oklahoma as an outgrowth of House Bill 1017.

More narrowly focused outcomes that stress basic skills "tend to cool the fire" of OBE opponents, Spady asserts. "Under OBE, you design your educational system around what you want students to demonstrate at the end" (Killackey, 1993).

Despite Spady's detailed defense of his curriculum plan, Fort Gibson and Hobart public schools pulled out of the project during the week Luksik was in the state. Lawton, Oklahoma's forty-two–building district, also put its 427-page Comprehensive Plan for 1993–1997 on hold because of attacks on the program's emphasis on self-esteem, self-motivation, and attitude improvement. Gwen Grey, mother of two children in the Lawton schools, said that she objects to the plan's numerous references to student behavior. Grey also insists that Lawton parents who share her concerns are not right-wing, conservative religious zealots. On the contrary, she said that inquiries have come from atheists, Democrats, Republicans, and liberals (Hutchinson, 1993, p. 15). Lawton Superintendent Dick Neptune said that a committee of parents and teachers for each of Lawton's forty-two schools had worked for months to develop individual plans with mission statements and exit outcomes—what students are expected to achieve before leaving. From those, a set of district outcomes was developed.

The Iowa debacle was even more conclusive. The Iowa Department of Education, directed by Dr. William Lepley, had over 200 educators working for two years developing a new education model. Again, this new model was called Outcome-Based Education. Critics considered it another state conspiracy to infuse social and political values into the curricula. Worse yet, some said that the state will eventually test children on values and give remedial lessons to those who fail (Siebert, 1993b). First, Lepley defended the goals, saying, "If people will be patient, we'll put something together that Iowans will be excited about and confident with." The counterattack by the Fundamentalists was swift and effective. "Alert Outcome-Based Education" pamphlets appeared in religious bookstores, calling the faithful to protest at state hearings. Parents for Traditional Choices groups were founded to ask for basic skills instead of OBE. "Stop Outcome-Based Education" bumper stickers were produced and sold well. In Davenport, a school board member sued the superintendent to see the test that would be used to measure a student's progress toward the outcomes. The Iowa State Education Association counterattacked in early April, using James Autry, a founder of People for the American Way.

Next, the department of education decided to reconsider the nine outcomes in light of mixed reviews. The process was to begin on March 1, be reviewed by the public in May, and be approved by the State Board in August (Knowles, 1993).

On May 6, the Iowa Department of Education abandoned its plan to establish statewide student performance goals. "I don't have enough support in the state to move it forward," Lepley said. He said that the department is not backing away from the outcomes philosophy or from insisting on higher expectations for Iowa students. But, instead of mandating statewide performance goals, the department would help school districts establish their own outcomes at the local level.

"Main Street Iowa questions whether Iowa schools—which regularly rank among the nation's best—need to undergo such dramatic changes," Lepley said. "But when I get with business groups and those who employ people, it's a different story. Business leaders are saying that Iowa students are graduating from high school without the skills needed to find a job in today's changing economy" (Siebert, 1993a) [4].

ONE SUPERINTENDENT FIGHTS BACK

Dr. Joe Drips is an Iowa administrator who, in two separate districts in the past decade, has met the various challenges of the Fundamentalists successfully. First in eastern Iowa at Central Community Schools of Clinton County and, more recently, at Southeast Polk Community School District (suburban Des Moines), Joe has used (1) Bill Cook's approach to strategic planning, (2) faith, and (3) "knowing your enemy" to meet every objection that the Christian Right has raised. Listen to him tell the story in his own words:

> At Central Community Schools, the attack was upon the potential adoption of a health curriculum document. At Southeast Polk, questions were raised about a new tax levy, and one in seven volunteer participants for a public community school strategic planning team were from conservative opinion. It is from this experience background that this writer has come to accept that you will not change the overall attitudes of members of conservative groups. However, you can impact their interpretation of your specific school's programs by using Bill Cook's strategic planning process and discipline and the "good will" for building consensus through inclusion. You can have a positive impact on those that question your programs.
>
> **Know yourself . . .**
>
> In both experiences, Central Community and Southeast Polk, one of the best defenses against attack was found to be knowledge of your own programs and expectations. In both experiences, greatest anxiety was caused when it was discovered that your "enemies" knew more detail about some aspects of your school program than you or your staff. Do not underestimate the resources of time, energy, and money that the conservative groups can throw at a public school issue. If you do, you will suddenly find yourself devoting full-time duty to attempts to simply slow their progress.
>
> Iowa's Human Growth and Development law requires that all parents be notified yearly of the classes and units that include

Human Growth and Development topics. This is to allow parents the option of removing their children from that specific instruction (removal is not an option for AIDS-related instruction). This is often the first time that an Iowa public school finds itself in front of questions from conservative groups. It does not matter that what is reported may be what has been taught, successfully, for many years without question. Once public notice is provided, conservative groups suddenly have a document to put in front of your total public that can be misinterpreted and used against you. Their ability to do this reflects an important truth. Like the Iowa Department of Education, we have failed to sufficiently communicate our message on these issues. We have simply relied on the public's "good will," without making use of it.

The movement to ask these questions is nationwide. The fact that you have not been questioned to date should not be interpreted as cause for feeling secure. Your time has just not come. It will.

Knowing yourself and your programs requires that you be ahead of the issue; understand everything that is included in your Human Growth and Development program; include various interest groups in its development; communicate that message to your public as it is developed and implemented; and remember that you represent the public schools. A democracy is said to "ameliorate the extremes in society." Conservative groups and their issues represent an extreme point of view. It is not your job to attempt to change their minds. You will not be successful. Your best hope is to make them a part of your discussion of programs, and let them see that they are not majority opinion and cannot subvert your programs based upon apathy of your general public.

Conservative groups pretend to want mainstream opinion to rule; they appeal to it. However, they know that it is in their best interest not to let mainstream opinion rule the day. They rely upon mainstream apathy to incite, misinform, and take over power structures like boards of education. However, you should remember that they do not represent current mainstream opinion. Many of their members have joined for questionable reasons. It is your job to point out the positive aspects of your school programs and that your programs represent, with proof, the mainstream opinion of your community. Conservative groups may make every effort to cloud that fact. Some of their group may also come to realize that they, too, can be comfortable with your approach.

The issue of "FAITH" is all important to both sides. In an attack on Human Growth and Development at Central Community Schools of Clinton County, a representative from Concerned Citizens for Education (CCE), when confronted with black and white truth that a claim made by William Coulson, Director of the Research Council on Ethnopsychology and nationally known opponent to the Lions' Quest Program, was not true, responded, "Well, if he thought it was true in his heart, it doesn't matter. It is still true." Another parent, when speaking about Quest, said, "He who teaches sin to the child shall burn in hell forever." Faith is a strong ally.

Dr. Robert Simonds, President of the National Association of Christian Educators/Citizens for Excellence in Education (CEE), knows its value. He states, "We need your 'faith' in God, to believe with us, for the great victories ahead. We must establish a CEE Christian parents chapter in every school district in America (15,700). We now have only 868. But that's a start—born of FAITH." Public school educators must remember "FAITH" and use it themselves. Their "FAITH" must center upon the fact that they are in the business of education because of their belief in doing good for others, because (in most cases) of their belief in some deity, their belief in the "common good," and their interest in helping. They must also have "FAITH" enough in the democratic process to use it for inclusion and consensus building in a public setting—democracy. It is through subversion—not application—of democracy that conservative groups prove successful.

Public educators' beliefs can cause a weakness if they do not know themselves, their personal belief structure or their school program's beliefs, when attacked. The educator will suddenly find himself/herself wondering how people could desire to attack and hurt someone like themselves, as nice as they are. Why? It is because someone needs to be the villain. Someone needs to be the unresponsive side. Someone needs to have evil in their heart. And to win over the vast majority of people that support public schools, conservative groups must have that "someone" that refuses to listen, to care, to change and to be responsive. It is important to isolate that someone from the group, attack and discredit. That someone is often the school superintendent, curriculum director, or other central office administrator.

That approach often causes a response of anger from central office staff. Therein lies a great danger. The attack states that you refuse to listen, to care, to change and to be responsive. The approach tries to isolate you so that you can provide no other response. The key to defusing the attack is to represent what you believe in before, during, and after the attack.

When the attack on Human Growth and Development became heated at Central Clinton, the high school principal was approached about a Department of Education-sponsored play, "Secrets," about AIDS and student sexual attitudes. The principal was concerned about presenting the play in the climate that existed, one of attack against public schools' understanding of decency and the potential adoption of our health curriculum guides. The principal was directed to review the school's mission statement and respond if the production was consistent with that mission. That mission statement read, "The mission of the Central Community School District of Clinton County, a community leader committed to excellence, is to educate the whole person to be a caring involved citizen in a global society." The response from the principal was "yes" and the play was presented. The CCE tried to mount an attack; it did not work. Central Clinton knew itself enough through Strategic Planning–developing beliefs, mission statements, parameters, objectives, and strategies–to fall back upon what it knew of itself and what it believed to save itself.

Another example comes from a church meeting organized to discuss the Human Growth and Development topic at Central Community Schools of Clinton County. During the question and answer portion, one CCE member asked, "Is it true that the word *penis* is included in the first grade spelling list?" Spelling lists were locally generated through school-developed curriculum. The school representative's response was that he did not believe that it was. The response was admittedly somewhat defensive to a point that caused reflection as days passed. The questioner had managed to isolate that the school representative did not know the answer to a curriculum question, and at the same time had made him appear to shy away from the educational issue involved. If the curriculum taught correct terms for body parts at the first grade level, what would there be to be defensive about the word *penis* being on the spelling list? Know yourself, your school program, and your community first. The Human Growth and Development health curriculum guide was adopted by the board of education with a 5–0 vote.

At Southeast Polk, a statewide organizer of a conservative group heard a presentation at a public hearing before the Iowa House of Representatives from a school representative. That presentation led to conservative questioning of an attempt to establish an instructional support tax levy in the district. That attempt required that no one petition to put the issue to a public vote. They had thirty days to petition after notice of intent to implement the levy. Upon visiting the central office, the conservative leader stated that he had reservations about additional taxing for public funds that would be spent on activities like Quest, and that he was thinking of starting a petition to stop this levy. An instructional time audit, produced in response to a state mandate, made it possible to show the questioner how little of the school's instructional time was devoted to this type of issue. It was less than 1 percent of the total elementary educational program. Knowing the truth about the program provided an answer to an attack that never materialized. Inclusion and willingness to talk, answer questions, preempted response. Having previously had contact with conservative groups also allowed this school representative to know the key words and how to defuse them. Not the least of those words was an understanding of the importance of commitment to stating that you are "a person of good will working for the common good" and soliciting equal response from the questioner.

Know your "enemy" . . .

There is a tendency to believe that everyone can be won over to reason. That is a dangerous assumption when dealing with conservative groups. Some of them are on a crusade. "Truth is not necessarily their ally." They may attempt to portray those that oppose their view as someone pushing perversion off on young people. The "good will" question is one that should be used with all public groups. It was generated through training sessions with Bill Cook's Strategic Planning process and discipline. It is the question of good will: "Are you a person of good will working for the common good?" It is a question that must be asked of all groups that approach the public school and its programs with questions, after it is made as a statement of "faith" by school representatives.

If a group, or its representatives, cannot answer in the affirmative, they are the "enemy" of public education. They are a group that you must fight. They will leave you no option. That does not mean that you will not include and attempt to reach consensus. You will treat them with the respect and dignity all patrons deserve. Knowing them to be your "enemy" allows you one defense you would not otherwise have. Expecting them to act as an "enemy" means that you expect them to attack and attempt to hurt. Knowing that ahead of time provides protection in your response. It will not lean toward emotion.

For example, Quest programs have been adopted by many school districts across the United States with the assistance of local Lions Clubs. The attack on Quest attempts to portray it as a meditation/mind-control instructional program designed to corrupt the nation's youth. The attack is vehement and distorted. Dr. Coulson portrays it as a "value free, affective" drug and sex education class. Perhaps the best type of response to this approach is one that we can all learn from. It shows a response that portrays knowledge of self and assurance of purpose: "It's laughable to assume that the leaders of the Lions Club would be the national sponsor of this without carefully checking it out (as would the school systems). What other sinister activities are the Lions involved in? Well, they open their meetings with a prayer, the Pledge of Allegiance, and a patriotic song."

It is the world's largest service organization—probably the world's largest contributor to cancer research and cancer-fighting equipment. Millions are spent yearly to provide leader dogs totally free to the blind. There's kidney dialysis, free vision clinics, hearing clinics, and partial or whole financing of ambulances or fire equipment. Locally, they assist the Salvation Army and sponsor Little League teams. The list goes on.

These are the things Quest and its Lions Club sponsors do. The question to the opponents should be, "What do you do?"

It is best to view those of the CEEs and CCEs that will not face "good will" test as your "enemy," not your friend, for two reasons. First, your friends will not treat you the way that these conservative groups will treat you. Second, their treatment is designed to elicit an emotional response. If you start your relationship understanding that you are dealing with an "enemy," you can grant them the dignity and respect that you give everyone, without the need to become emotional and weaker in their eyes. You can concentrate on the fact that you are the person of "good will working for the common good."

Understanding that some seen as "enemies" are simply questioners that want answers . . .

It is important also to understand that some of the people asking you questions are simply people of "good will" seeking answers. While it is true that they may start seeking answers after they were misinformed by people from conservative groups, they are not part of the conservative groups. This is important to remember for at least two reasons. One, you need these people; they may make up the majority of your school district. Normally, they ask too few questions: it is refreshing to face their questions. After all, you are a person of "good will working for the common good." These people must be treated with dignity, respect, and understanding so that they can support your programs. They will be the very people that will eventually see through the attack of the conservative groups for what it is, a movement founded by religious zealots intent on destroying public education and founding a theocracy instead of democracy. The second reason you must remember is that these people need dignified answers; you are the professional in this discussion. Professional ethics demand that you be the person that recognizes: ". . . responsibility for explaining and interpreting . . . professional principles and actions when

One Superintendent Fights Back   55

reasonable questions arise, whether from colleagues, students, community or the profession as a whole."

We often pay lip service in education to having parental and public involvement in what we do. Many in the conservative groups have discovered several facts about our statements. They understand, first of all, that in most cases we do very little to foster and seek that input. They also understand that since many of us do not foster and seek that input, but say we want it, they can use their energy and activism to use our own words against us. They will provide involvement, like we say we want. They will seek election to boards of education. They will review books and media to see that it is appropriate. They will follow through with challenges to instructional materials. They will volunteer in great numbers to participate on school committees. All of this will happen at the same time that they, too, rely on public apathy to become involved. This reliance allows them to control the agenda. It allows them to place people on the board of education. Your ally is full community involvement. Involvement is the conservative group's tool for control; full community involvement is also your community's tool to keep possession of your public school in the public hands. Use it as your tool. Do not give it away.

The power of inclusion, consensus, and the statement of good will . . .

This approach provides a strong means to defuse conservative groups, foster faith in school programs, help you better understand yourself, your "enemies," and your publics. All of these items are included in Bill Cook's approach to strategic planning. One good example of the power of this approach is found in the experience at Southeast Polk. When volunteers were asked to fill a community strategic planning team, it was soon obvious that about 17 percent of the respondents were from a conservative background. They questioned Quest. They questioned Outcome-Based Education. They questioned environmental education.

There was initial cause for concern that this type of population could lead to stalemate in a process—strategic planning—that requires consensus on all issues. Contacts with people involved with strategic planning suggested that reliance should be placed on the power of the strategic planning process and discipline. Inclusion was better than exclusion. It was with great care and concern that the strategic planning session began with a statement of introduction required of all participants. Everyone was informed of the point that a democracy "ameliorates the extremes of society." Everyone was required to introduce themselves and prepare for the consensus building process by making a pledge that they were "people of good will working for the common good." In a public situation, preparing to develop a strategic plan for a public school, it was difficult to refuse to make such a pledge. Even more so, it would be difficult not to fulfill such a pledge. That pledge makes it possible to align your publics to face the issue of whether someone is your "enemy" or someone is your "patron." It draws a line in the sand that is difficult to cross. And it is a line that it is important to draw.

Two members of the thirty-member strategic planning team were home schoolers; they chose to keep their children out of the public schools. Yet they were expected to, and did, contribute to the strengthening of a public school system. They even participated in a listing of challenges to the public schools' competition that included home schooling as an issue to be faced and dealt with. In every respect, although their opinions were different than the majority point of view, they were able to provide input that helped everyone better understand the mission of our public school.

The end result of the process was one of inclusion that developed an understanding of all parties. The strongest statements that came with support of the home schooling point of view were: ". . . that the family unit is the primary influence in the development of the individual," ". . . no historical writings will be excluded purely on religious grounds," and ". . . parental/community involvement should not be discouraged." They were countered with statements like: ". . . that the family, community and social institutions all contribute to conditions of success," and ". . . nothing will interfere with a student's right to learn and a teacher's right to teach." All statements led to consensus, including, "We will not tolerate graduation of a student not meeting district outcomes."

One modification of the process was the statement to the team, by the facilitator, that any minority opinion may some day become the majority opinion. Any idea that could not be discussed in a large group, because it could not reach consensus in a small group, would be allowed for presentation at the end of the process. It would not be part of the strategic plan, but it could be discussed by the group. None took the opportunity to address any issue. All understood the strength of mainstream opinion, strengthened further by free and open debate on all issues. Many spoke in praise of the community feeling they had developed in the process.

"Bad news on the doorstep" comes from Don Maclean's classic Rock and Roll song "American Pie." It goes on to talk about, "The day the music died." Well, rock and roll did not die at Clear Lake, with a plane crash in a winter storm. It is probable that Iowa's Outcome-Based Education did not die with Dr. William Lepley's movement away from state level outcomes. Communication can make it possible to make educational leaders serve their communities in a manner that allows questions from "enemies" and "patrons" lead to a community discussion that allows the best to be presented for all. The open admission that the state-level approach to Outcome-Based Education was not appropriately presented to the public can serve as the catalyst to not making the same mistake at the local level. As with strategic planning, it is possible to bring people of divergent views together and to develop a consensus on where the public schools should go, as long as all the people are "people of good will working for the common good." Indeed, some of the people that left Southeast Polk's strategic planning sessions still felt that Outcome-Based Education is not the appropriate approach, but that Southeast Polk's interpretation of Outcome-Based Education was acceptable. Note the high number of people who rate their own school districts as excellent when they claim that the nation's school systems are in danger of disintegration. It is knowledge, acceptance, and understanding that lead to acceptance. Many of the conservative groups' members often feel disenfranchised. Letting them in, with a pledge of "good will working for the common good" is one way to make them a part of the team. Reminding ourselves of the need to keep the good will pledge as "faith" cements the team concept. In some instances, that may be enough to make it possible to accomplish what public education needs—communication.

PREPARATION TIPS

Whether you prepare teachers, counselors, or administrators or serve as one, the ability to identify and deal with attacks by the Religious Right is an essential skill component for your program. Many of us in higher education will also be fending off our own attackers regarding politically correct language, diversity, and curriculum content. Experience and the growing research literature on the anti-reform movement suggests:

1. Study the *Protection of Pupil Rights Statute* (Hatch Amendment). The Religious Right has distributed thousands of sample letters that stretch far beyond the federal statute's intentions. These letters are used to threaten lawsuits on loss of federal revenues to school systems.
2. Ensure that your faculty and all those you prepare know the Religious Right's beliefs, targets, tactics and objectives.

3. Teach your students the concepts of censorship, academic freedom, and constitutional rights.
4. Prepare your students to use meaningful parental involvement practices. We need their wealth of experience, wisdom, and support—not just items for a bake sale.
5. Teach alternatives to OBE as curriculum renewal, alignment, and assessment practices. *Design down and plan up* sounds good in the OBE manual, but the process takes so long that the activists of the Religious Right have too much time to set up their big guns.
6. Use Joe Drips' idea regarding the strength of your district's educational goals and vision. If there is no clear alignment between the district's vision and a program, you're going to be in trouble. Teachers and administrators need time and training to be able to articulate why they use curricula and teaching materials.
7. Teach procedures for handling conflict. Schools need established protocols for disruptive behavior, filibusters, videotaping, attacks on personnel, and "on-the-spot" legal demands by activists.
8. Finally, approach First Amendment rights of students, faculty, parents, and other members of the community with patience and respect. Freedom of speech cuts both ways. Don't assume that elementary and secondary teachers have the same rights to academic freedom as do university and college professors. The courts have been very clear in that regard. Many patrons who raise questions about proposed curriculum content and methods changes are simply trying to help you provide better schools for their children.

Stealth candidates and critics have the ability to "fly under the radar of common sense and fair play." If you and your students are "walking the talk" of balance and reason, the majority of any community will support the long overdue reform of renewed curriculum and high standards.

ENDNOTES

1. Radio and television shows are a new way to study political ideas, movements, and strategies. Certainly, Mr. Perot and President Clinton have used

such outlets to great advantage. Unfortunately, they (the shows) come at an awkward time for educators to monitor and you can't get a synopsis from a clipping service (yet!).
2. The Citizens for Excellence in Education is trying to prove that there is a national pattern of entrapment whereby children are asked affective psychological questions about their family or personal life. Their literature explains, "We need to file at least five regional lawsuits on entrapment to prove the national connection." Naturally, such entrapment would have to be done without the parent's knowledge. Such a potential mess can be avoided by always obtaining parental permission for such surveys, but counselors and other educators often get in a hurry to gather data to justify funding proposals or simply to satisfy someone's need for a thesis or dissertation.
3. Our urban readers may not be aware of PETA, *P*eople United for the *E*thical *T*reatment of *A*nimals, but Iowa livestock growers are. The PETA philosophy includes vegetarianism; thus many cattlemen found the Republican plank to be attractive.
4. The other shoe fell on May 24. Lepley sent a letter to all Iowa school districts announcing that henceforth the Iowa Department of Education would no longer be involved with the Global Education Resource Catalog. "This decision is in keeping with the Department's emphasis on leadership in student achievement, assessment, staff development and other broad areas and de-emphasis on development of materials for classroom use," he wrote. Later, Lepley resigned to become headmaster of the Hershey (PA) Independent School.

REFERENCES

Brookhiser, R. 1993. "The Cultural Right Is Here to Stay," *Time*, 141(22):74.
Cloudwalker, C. 1993. "Thermopolis Group Protests 'Outcome-Based' Curriculum," *Casper State Tribune* (September 18):2.
Dillon, S. 1993. "Light School Board Vote Really Was Heaviest Ever," *The New York Times* (May 18):A12.
Eakman, B. K. 1990. *Educating for the "New World Order."* Costa Mesa, CA: Citizens for Excellence in Education, P.O. Box 3200, 92628.
Flansburg, J. 1993. "Education's Real Problem," *The Des Moines Register* (Tuesday, June 1):13A.
1993. "The Generation That Forgot God," *Time* (April 15):44–48.
Howse, B. 1991. *The New Age Is Not So New*. Concepts of Truth, P.O. Box 24062, St. Paul, MN 55125.
Hutchinson, M. A. 1993. "Parents Oppose Personal Aspects of Lawton Teaching Plan," *The Sunday Oklahoman* (May 9):A15.
Iowa State Education Association. 1993. "Schools under Siege," *ISEA Communique* (February):6–7.
Jones, J. L. 1993. "Targets of the Right," *The American School Board Journal* (April): 22–29.
Killackey, J. 1993. "Education Methods Debated Statewide," *The Sunday Oklahoman* (May 9):1.

Knowles, M. S. 1993. "The Outcomes Are Dead, Not," *Thrust Newsletter*, Iowa ASCD, 11(4):4.

Mydans, S. 1993. "A Political Proving Ground for a Rising Religious Right," *The New York Times* (February 20):1.

1993. "The Perfect School," *U.S. News and World Report* (January 11):114(1): 46–60.

1993. "Religious Right Targets Education," *The American School Board Journal* (April):9.

Siebert, M. 1993a. "Statewide Education Goals Dropped," *The Des Moines Register* (May 7):1:

Siebert, M. 1993b. "Teaching Based on Outcome under Fire," *The Des Moines Register* (March 22):9A.

Simonds, K. 1991. *A Critique of America 2000: An Education Strategy*. Costa Mesa, CA: Citizens for Excellence in Education, P.O. Box 3200, 92628.

CHAPTER 3
Why Are the Fundamentalists So Unhappy with Public Schools?

FUNDAMENTALISTS view school reform as a communistic threat! Members of the Religious Right continue to hammer away at the "collectivist-learning reforms" of Outcome-Based Education, which, in their view, is the product of edu-zealots who have co-opted the language of traditionalists by insisting on "standards" and "outcomes." Wouldn't parents want such things—results and accountability? Listen to Michelle Malkin, who writes for the *Los Angeles Daily News:*

> ...That's not what OBE is really all about.
>
> The outcomes do not tell you what students know and when, like whether they've mastered multiplication tables by second grade, can identify the 50 states on a map of the United States in third grade, or explain the plot and major themes of *The Adventures of Huckleberry Finn* by seventh grade.
>
> In fact, a staple of OBE reform is to do away with report cards—those antiquated, self-esteem–destroying documents. Instead, OBE gurus and other "educational reformers" prefer to measure academic progress with a checklist of social attitudes and behaviors. The outcomes they've designed measure things like "the tendency to subordinate personal desire to the public good" and whether students "understand the views and needs of others." (Malkin, 1993)

The defeat of Iowa's plan for OBE was reported in the last chapter. The Pennsylvania plan for OBE became state policy—but not before a bruising battle led by Peg Luksik, a Johnstown resident who became the "mother of the outcomes revolt" (Harp, 1993). Luksik and her allies put state officials on notice that school reforms aimed at guaranteeing that every child will master each subject and, in the process, learn an appreciation of certain state-defined values, will face a fight.

The compromise worked out by the Pennsylvania Department of Education and the legislature has pared the final list of outcomes to fifty-three from an original list of 127 basic outcomes and 448 subordinate outcomes.

OBE fared even less well in Virginia. Virginia, like Iowa, had a two-year study to determine outcomes for high school graduates. The Christian Coalition, headed by Ralph E. Reed, Jr., is based in Chesapeake, Virginia, and did a not-so-subtle job on the project. Governor Douglas Wilder, in September 1993, directed the Virginia Department of Education to withdraw plans to implement OBE in the state's public schools.

Both sides have accused the other of being underhanded, or misquoting opposition positions, and of reading research findings "out of context." Educators charge that ultraconservatives are using "stealth" campaign tactics to gain control of local and state school boards of education. The conservative religious leaders counter that the real stealth candidates are liberal incumbents who talk one way to get elected and then vote the opposite way. In truth, by January of 1994 a big picture emerged, and both sides had lost any "under the radar" stealth advantage.

First, religious Fundamentalists were succeeding in using the democratic process to block some public policy issues by protest. Second, they were moving from the pulpit to the soap box to the ballot box to gain the power to reshape public policy.

While there are no definitive figures, officials with the Christian Fundamentalist organization Citizens for Excellence in Education claim that more than 4500 "parents with conservative family values" have been elected to school boards since 1989. Nationwide, there are 96,000 school board members.

> The liberal advocacy group, People for the American Way, which monitors the activity of the religious right across the country, has identified 243 religious conservatives who ran for local school boards in primaries or general elections in 1992–1993, and about one-third were successful in their campaigns. (Arocha, 1993)

Third, the people who oppose "liberalism" in public education did not always have a clear label or a visible connection with groups such as the Christian Coalition or Citizens for Excellence in Education, but you can be sure their opposition centers on common themes, e.g., sex education, self-esteem, and programs that emphasize independent thinking. They have discovered that school board elections are the easiest way to get started in political power because such elections require little in the way of campaign funds, draw few voters, and attract little attention from the media until the election is almost over.

WHAT DO THEY WANT?

Probably the best answer to that question is "for someone to listen!" Education professors and their products, superintendents, principals, teachers, and consultants, may not like the message very much.

Ultraconservative board members and like-thinking parents want to influence educational policy and statewide leadership on issues such as Outcome-Based Education, health, and sex education programs. Their theme is becoming unified: local control in education, parents' rights, and strong, factual academics. They argue that their points are valid. Outcome-Based Education is "experimental and costly." Statewide goals would emphasize "values and beliefs and deemphasize academics." They argue that health and sex education is an open door for health clinics to bypass both family responsibility and the rights of parents to know what is going on with their children.

Where conservatives have taken over a school district, their actions also give some insight into their intentions. According to a report issued by People for the American Way in July 1993, Religious Right members hold the majority on five United States school boards, viz., New Berlin, Wisconsin; Round Rock, Texas; Duval County, Florida; Lake County, Florida; and Vista, California, a suburb of San Diego. The Vista board first tackled the issues of opening their meetings with an invocation and whether to hire four attorneys who have Christian views. They approved prayer as an opening exercise but did not hire the attorneys. Vista also has included Biblical Creationism (called *Intelligent Design Theory*) in the curriculum.

Round Rock, Texas, is a racially diverse, bedroom community adjacent to Austin. Last spring (1993), the newly elected conservative majority voted five to one (with one member not present) to allow prayer at graduation. Later this year, the board is expected to consider whether the district's counselors are to drop the use of Pumsey. This program, which uses a puppet to teach self-esteem, has been attacked by some parents in the district for teaching children secular values.

Robert Simonds, President of Citizens for Excellence in Education, puts what they want very bluntly in an invited article in a recent issue of the AASA's *Administrator:* "Please work with us or you will force us to abandon you" (Simonds, 1993). Simonds, using an "in your face" approach to open his piece, raises the interest of superintendents by describing the recently fired superintendents of New York City and Los Angeles as losers in a cultural war:

> ... Look at the New York schools' fallen schools chancellor (who promoted the idea that young children should learn about homosexuality) or at Los Angeles, where another top school chief went down in ignominy in 1991 because of "Mission SOAR," a new age, occult curriculum.
>
> What causes these mid-career debacles by otherwise intelligent educational leaders? The answer is, of course, both simple and complex.
>
> It's simple in that a good dose of higher order thinking skills, more commonly known as common sense, would help. It's complex because of the often irrational influence of left-wing educational radicals whose agenda is a socialist, anti-Christian diatribe designed to denigrate all religions, but especially Christianity. (Simonds, 1993, p. 19)

Simonds continues, "For most Americans, and certainly for me, forcing the left wing educational extremists' agenda upon our innocent school children is unacceptable. I believe the agenda soon will be history."

After complaining that local superintendents and boards have been begged to consider a mutually acceptable solution to their complaints, Simonds says only a few superintendents listen. The rest, he says, tell parents, "We have a model school—you are the only one who has complained." He lists the usual ploys. (1) We can't change our curriculum every time a parent comes in here;

we would be changing it a dozen times a week. (2) Trust us. We know what's best for your child. We are trained professionals. (3) Don't give in. If you give an inch, they'll take a mile.

Simonds makes a clear threat. School districts that send teachers and administrators to seminars on "How to Stop Fundamentalists in Education" are going to be targeted by secular and conservative parent groups through tax rebellion and lawsuits. Why not, he says. Wouldn't that rightly happen if the seminar focused on "How to Stop African-American Influence on Education?" He rhetorically asks, "Should we conclude that the National Education Association, People for the American Way and school districts that send representatives to their bigoted Christophobic gatherings are as bad as the Ku Klux Klan?"

It's clear that Simonds believes his organization speaks for all Christians when he counterattacks the spate of "how to cope" seminars:

> Citizens for Excellence in Education has some questions about this hate-mongering activity:
> 1. Are those who attend these sessions the same school people who espouse pluralism, cultural diversity, religious freedom, and parental inclusion?
> 2. Are children being taught that Christians are dangerous?
> 3. Are Christians acting illegally or undemocratically by electing parents to school boards?
> 4. What's all this talk about balancing our school boards? Is there a Christian balance on your district's board? (Simonds, 1993, p. 22)

Simonds marshals a long list of church membership data to conclude that Christians are not a minority, that there are about sixty parents for every teacher in the public schools, and cautions the NEA that parents—not teachers—have the voting power. Assuming his figures are accurate, Citizens for Excellence in Education (CEE) has 1350 chapters with 185,000 active parents with a little more than a million "standby" parents. (Simonds' quote marks. I'm not sure what a standby parent is.)

CEE presently has more than 800 churches operating Public School Awareness Committees to keep parents informed. Their goal is ten churches (and committees) in every school district and one local CEE parent chapter in every school district.

Simonds insists that CEE has a simple agenda: (1) to return academic excellence to our schools, (2) to return moral sanity and family values to our schools, and (3) to elect parents to community and statewide boards who will hire parent-sensitive superintendents when these boards don't listen.

> CEE wants an academic schedule with goals similar to the National Commission on Excellence in Education's *A Nation at Risk*. Billions have been spent on school reform nationally only to see more affective (psychological, new age, homosexual) agendas take precedence over academics. Parents want to keep the SAT as our national assessment test. (Simonds, 1993, pp. 21–22)

"Outcome-Based Education is doomed to failure," Simonds argues, "not because it's a bad idea, but because the name is a smoke screen for an ever more liberal agenda of undefined outcomes, opening a Pandora's box." He wants maintenance of local control and traditional American values. The focus should be all on an academic environment in which teachers teach, rather than just facilitate. Schools must develop a racial, multicultural, American melting pot theory according to Simonds and maintain school discipline and character development classes [1].

Simonds ends his essay with a promise of hope for school administrators and a swipe at professors. He boasts that CEE, along with Christian Coalition, Concerned Women for America, EXCEL, and others, obtained 960,000 signatures to put the school choice initiative on the November 1993 ballot in California. He claims, "If we win, school leaders will also be winners. You will be set free from the bondage of the NEA monopoly on education" (Simonds, 1993, p. 22).

Simonds believes that curriculum specialists and administrators have fallen prey to special interest groups and "university eggheads" who live and thrive on publishing wild ideas.

FACTORS IN THE FRAY

In the past, a common question raised when groups are discussing the problems of gays in the miliary or on a college campus was, "You know anyone who is gay?" Not surprisingly, the answer was often, "No, do you?" The closet is more open now, at least on campus. Similarly, a quest for a conservative professor in most departments in a large public university drew blank looks even a couple of years ago. Even this year's annual meeting of the Organization of American Historians lamented that the topic of American Conservatism has largely been neglected.

What Is Conservatism?

"While studies of conservative intellectual and political movements have appeared more frequently in the past few years, the topic has still not received anything like the attention from historians that its role in American politics suggests it should" (Winkler, 1993, p. A6).

The conservative tradition in America has been difficult for scholars to characterize for several reasons. Alan Brinkley, a professor of history at Columbia University, says conservatism seems more a cluster of sometimes contradictory ideas than a coherent ideology (Winkler, 1993, p. A7). It developed as a major political force only in the last twenty years, when it was just associated with a Western (United States) regionalism that most historians thought to be unimportant. More importantly, American conservatism in most of the twentieth century rested on philosophical foundations that were not much different from the liberal tradition. The individual versus the government used to be considered a *liberal* concept.

Conservatism was viewed as a futile dissent against modernization. The assumption was made that modern liberal society has become ever more rational, progressive, and secular. Modern conservatism has trashed that assumption.

To make the increasing popularity of conservatism even more confounding to the scholar and the public school educator, modern conservatism includes a criticism of relativism and a defense of timeless moral and intellectual truths *(eternal verities)*. Rising religious Fundamentalism took most liberals by surprise.

What is especially difficult to understand for the male school superintendent trying so hard to be politically correct is the incongruity between conservative thought and the material interests of conservative women. Women seem to have so much to lose from the antifeminism of the conservative movement.

Perhaps the most confusing part of conservatism for liberal school administrators to grasp is that right-wing politics can accommodate tangential cultural issues and social networks. Community values and social reform extend far beyond the Republican Party. That's probably why the establishment (present school board members and superintendents and their NEA teacher colleagues) are so quick to charge "stealth candidate." Not all conservatives look like Phyllis Schlafly or talk like Jerry Falwell!

United States Culture of Complaint

In the previous chapter on the Religious Right, I claimed that part of our problem with the issues raised by OBE was that no one was listening to others. Civility, tolerance, and pluralism seem to have left this country as they have Yugoslavia.

Recently, Robert Hughes, an Australian citizen, published a book that addresses the "New National Business." Hughes, in his book, *Culture of Complaint: The Fraying of American,* pulls back far enough to discover that the United States right wing's religious fundamentalism and the left wing's politically correct (PC) movement are cut from the same cloth (Hughes, 1993).

He asks, how could Americans, a formerly freedom-loving people, replace their passion for independence with an urge to nitpick one another? When did we decide that the Constitution—along with freedom of religion, press, and speech—promises us freedom from having our feelings hurt and freedom from unpleasantness? It seems that Americans, with too much time and money on our hands, now find it easy to discover obscenity, discrimination, and esteem looseness everywhere.

There is a sort of ideal symbiosis in the politically correct/ Religious Right clash. Where, Hughes asks, would the editors of *American Spectator* or the contributors to the *New Criterion* be without the inexhaustible flow of PC claptrap from the academic left?

America has a long history of curbing freedom in order to preserve liberty. Hughes cites Jesse Helms' defeated attempt to force the National Endowment of the Arts to fund only *nice* art. "Under the Helms amendment," he writes, "a fire worshipper might even claim that the presence of a fire extinguisher in the museum offends *his* god."

The attacks on OBE (and many of the defense statements) are clearly examples of the "Culture of Complaint." Tom Kelly, in his monthly column for *The Effective School Report,* tries to sort this out:

> There is a growing confusion and criticism of OBE across our country. This is slowing the progress of OBE in many areas, and therefore needs to be addressed.
>
> In the most basic sense, OBE represents a shift in the focus of education. Until recently, education focused primarily on instruction or teaching. In fact, every state has laws requiring evaluation of teachers. We now realize that teaching is only a means. The end is learning, or results, or outcomes. This shift in focus is appropriate and necessary. What is taught and how is secondary. What is learned, and how well, is primary.
>
> Other than clarifying the categorical confusion (i.e., ends-means) OBE does not espouse any specific values. Schools and school districts decide the outcomes to be learned, just as they have always decided the material to be taught. Communities in our country vary tremendously, from the ridiculous to the sublime. The outcomes they choose for their students will vary accordingly. (Kelly, 1993, p. 1)

Kelly says of criticism that OBE teaches values, "We must recognize that schools have always taught values—good or bad. Whether OBE is used to teach healthy values or not is a function of how people use it." He concludes that the values that critics have attached to OBE—sex education, use of condoms, secularism—are going on in schools that have never considered OBE.

The argument has been made that all truly great teachers instill values in students. Yet many argue that in *public* schools, a teacher should not instill his or her values in students. The best answer to that comes from an anecdote told about the legendary mathematics teacher in Los Angeles, Jaime Escalante. Escalante says he seeks every opportunity to impose his ethic of "achievement, success, and hard work" on his students. In response to the question, "Why force your values on them?" Escalante fires back: "Because my values are better than theirs."

Differences over What to Do

Leaders and groups in the Religious Right believe that most proposals to improve public education since the publication of *A Nation at Risk,* ten years ago, are wrong and dangerous. Part of the misunderstanding comes from the official pronouncements of high-level national spokespersons—such as Bush or Clinton and Secretaries of Education. Recently, John Goodlad has written that there are actually two different reform movements: one "official" and policy-driven, centralized top-down, and mostly rhetorical; the other, less visible and teacher-driven, decentralized bottom-up, and often quite substantive.

Conservatives hear the rhetoric of OBE leaders, and it drives them wild! Worse yet, OBE has become such a broad umbrella that any new idea, however untested, can be "shaded." At the root of Outcome-Based Education is the desire to raise student achievement and convince the nation's schools to fix their sights on what children learn rather than what teachers teach and what the curricula describe. The actual programs, however, stray far from such concise goals. Talk to any state's leaders proposing OBE and you hear "restructured schools" that will eschew the present focus on regulations and credit hours; "goal-driven" schools that put the major emphasis on goals and outcomes as carrots to inspire innovation; and "improvement for all," the mastery learning piece of OBE intended to use a test/teach/test/reteach approach meant to bring all students up to mastery levels in each subject.

Bill Spady must feel very frustrated when he compares what he has been teaching school leaders for over ten years regarding OBE and what is actually done. When OBE moved from the grass-roots to the state level about three years ago, the fat was in the fire. If a state used the term OBE, it became a lightning rod for protest. In places like Kentucky, the buzzword OBE was never mentioned, but its influence can be seen in new performance-based assessments and reform concepts meant to focus less on process and more on student achievement. Illinois has even had praise from Pennsylvania's most outspoken OBE critics regarding that state's program because the focus is more narrow, i.e., standards for achievement in language arts, mathematics, science, social studies, and writing. Goals are set but not measured in physical health and the arts.

The Right probably likes the Illinois program because it looks like an accountability model, not OBE. The Illinois plan measures schoolwide performance, sets improvement targets, and then helps schools that fall below expectations.

David Leo-Nyquist believes that if teachers could make an imprint on the reform movement, it would be more acceptable to conservatives and would be more effective:

> The bumper sticker adage, "Think globally, act locally" is relevant here. We have always acted locally: that's the nature of our daily hands-on work with kids in classrooms. But, few of us school people have spent much time "thinking globally" about what we do: trying to understand how our work fits in to the "big picture" of educational policy and national trends. Unfortunately, that has been both a responsibility we have never taken on and a power that others (usually policy makers many times removed from the day-to-day realities of schools and classrooms) have assumed *for* us. (Leo-Nyquist, 1993, p. 1)

Perceptions of How Bad It Is

The 1993 Phi Delta Kappa/Gallup education poll released September 28 registered the largest one-year improvement in the grades given by the public to the local public schools. Almost half of the respondents (47%) awarded their local public schools grades of A or B, a gain of seven percentage points from the previous year and the highest percentage since the 48 percent recorded when the question was first asked in 1974 (Phi Delta Kappa, 1993, p. 1). The announcement was little noticed.

The bigger headlines are provided for reports of parent groups organizing to stop reform plans. In Kansas, a new battleground for OBE, the headlines read, "Parents Groups Battling over Schools' Soul"; "*New Age* Reform Plan Seen as Primary Evil." Outcome-Based Education in Kansas is known by the formal title, *Quality Performance Accreditation*. Accreditation is based on

The following are brief sketches of the major conservative religious-oriented groups involved in influencing public school governance. The information was provided by the AASA's *School Administrator* from a summary compiled by the People for the American Way.

American Family Association
(P.O. Box 2440, Tupelo, MS 38803)

Founded in 1977, this association is involved in public school censorship, particularly regarding the elementary school textbook series, Impressions. The association has filed lawsuits to ban the text on the grounds it "promotes the religion of witchcraft."

Membership estimates vary between 89,000 and 600,000, with 650 local chapters nationwide. The 1992 budget was $7 million. The Rev. Donald Wildmon serves as president.

Christian Coalition
(P.O. Box 1990, Chesapeake, VA 23320)

Founded by Pat Robertson in 1989, this powerful political force is working to elect "Christian candidates" to school boards nationwide. The organization runs leadership schools in most states to train potential candidates.

Membership is about 350,000 with 727 local chapters. The annual budget is about $410 million. Ralph Reed, Jr. serves as executive director.

Citizens for Excellence in Education
(P.O. Box 3200, Costa Mesa, CA 92628)

Founded in 1983, this is one of the most active groups challenging books, educational materials, and curricula, especially those dealing with drug abuse prevention and self-esteem. The group also wants to rid schools of textbooks mentioning the theory of evolution. The organization helps its members get elected to school boards. The group publishes a bimonthly newsletter, *Education Newsline.*

Membership is estimated at 130,000 with 1210 local chapters. Robert Simonds serves as president.

Concerned Women for America
(370 L'Enfant Promenade S.W., Suite 800, Washington, D.C. 20024)

Founded in 1979, this organization fights against sex education curricula that are not abstinence-based and opposes anti-drug and alcohol programs that emphasize self-esteem. The group provides its materials to those challenging books in public schools.

Membership is estimated at 600,000 with 1200 chapters. The annual budget is about $10 million. Beverly LaHaye is the president.

FIGURE 3.1 Profiles of far-right citizens' groups.

Eagle Forum
(P.O. Box 618, Alton, IL 62002)

Founded in 1972, the organization opposes AIDS education, sex education that is not strictly abstinence-only, and self-esteem programs. The group publishes a monthly newsletter, *Education Reporter,* and its materials are frequently cited by local censors of school texts.
Membership is about 80,000. Phyllis Schlafly serves as president.

Focus on the Family
(P.O. Box 35500, Colorado Springs, CO 80935)

Founded in 1977, this organization opposes sex education programs that are not strictly abstinence-only and runs seminars across the country to help evangelical Christians become involved in politics. The group has an extensive publications program and radio and television shows.
Membership is estimated at 2 million. The annual budget is about $477 million. James C. Dodson is the president.

Traditional Values Coalition
(100 S. Anaheim Blvd., Suite 320, Anaheim, CA 92805)

Founded in 1981, this organization opposes the teaching of evolution and sex education that does not exclude information about birth control and disease prevention. The group forced a delay in the congressional confirmation of former San Diego superintendent Thomas Payzant as assistant secretary of the U.S. Department of Education.
Membership includes 15,000 churches, about half of them in California. The Rev. Louis Sheldon is chair.

FIGURE 3.1 (continued) Profiles of far-right citizens' groups.

student performance and not simply by inputs of programs and dollars.

> Many of those opposing school reform say it opens the door to programs rooted in New Age philosophies and Satanism, which they say teach children to defy their parents. Education experts argue that the term *New Age* is simply an updated version of attacks on *secular humanism,* a '70s phrase used to describe a philosophy that looked to man, not God, as the authority. (Thomas, 1992, p. 1A)

The charge is that the United States public schools have abandoned the basic skills. Ralph Reed, Jr., who speaks for Pat Robertson's Christian Coalition, says, "We believe curriculum must return to the basics—reading, writing and performance of basic mathematics skills have been whittled away by values clarification, human sexuality courses and Outcome-Based Education" [2].

According to the U.S. Department of Education, only 25 percent of eighth graders in the United States are proficient in mathematics. Two-thirds of high school seniors cannot name the decade in which the Civil War was fought or the half century in which Columbus discovered America.

This knowledge is essential to good citizenship and to a future work force that can compete in an international economy. The one simple standard that should govern curriculum decisions is: will it help students learn to read, write, and perform basic math skills? (Reed, 1993, p. 18)

The most interesting clash of perceptions is that of desirability of choice. The latest Phi Delta Kappa/Gallup Poll of *The Public Attitudes Towards the Public Schools* indicates strong support for choice programs within the public schools, but strong opposition to allowing parents to choose a private school for their children to attend at public expense. Sixty-five percent of the respondents favored choice across all schools of a community that were public. Almost three-quarters (74 percent) said no to choice of a private school at public expense. Nothing in the data suggests that the public is becoming more receptive to voucher plans. Phi Delta Kappa, in the education fraternity's news release, believes the new findings partly explain the defeat of the Colorado voucher plan last year (1993).

In November, 1994, Californians rejected Proposition 174, a $2500 per year voucher that can be used in private schools for each school-age child in a family. At present, approximately 12 percent of the nation's children are in private schools. In California, the figure is 14 percent.

In late summer, George Will began citing an unusual "choice" statistic in his nationally syndicated column (Will, 1993). He repeated the statistic a few days later on "This Week with David Brinkley." He said, "Nationally, about half of all urban public school teachers send their children to private schools." This figure is so out of whack that Gerald Bracey in his *Commentary* Op. Ed. column for *Education Week* called it another urban legend on a par with crocodiles in the sewers of New York City (1993). Mr. Bracey did a little checking and discovered that the estimate of 50 percent probably came from the Institute for Justice, the Cato Institute, and the American Enterprise Institute. Bracey concluded that 21 percent is probably the most accurate estimate available.

Several of the sources that Bracey contacted to check on Will's estimate were conservative school critics and ardent advocates of school choice. The original source of data, the American Enterprise Institute, excused George Will's 50 percent figure as "a bit of an overstatement." Bracey retorted, "A *bit* of an overstatement? The kind of exaggeration contained in Mr. Will's remark is the kind of an exaggeration that turned Pinocchio's nose into a jousting lance!"

The Christian Coalition uses a different set of statistics but comes to the same conclusion. Listen to Reed:

> *We believe school choice will improve public education by introducing healthy competition.*
>
> Surveys show 70 percent of the American people favor the right to choose the best schools for their child. Those who know the public schools best know the effectiveness of choice. An estimated 22 percent of public school teachers send their children to private schools—twice the national average. Among school teachers in Chicago, more than 40 percent opt for private or parochial schools.
>
> A school choice initiative will be on the ballot in California next month. As with the tax limitation movement and the success of Proposition 13, a victory in California could sweep across the country like a prairie fire. (Reed, 1993, p. 18)

Advances in the Understanding of the Nature of Cognitive Competence

There has been a revolution in the social sciences in the past twenty years. The revolution has been our knowledge of the nature of cognitive competence and the long path that leads to its attainment. This new knowledge tells us much about how we should create curricula, teach, and assess student performance. In psychology, the once firmly entrenched behaviorism of Thorndyke, Watson, Hull, Spense, and Skinner has given way to several generations of "mind as information processing system" (Gardner, 1987).

Research in cognitive and skills learning has dramatic importance to curriculum design, delivery, and assessment. Unfortunately, the Religious Right has almost no knowledge of this revolution, and practicing private school teachers have little more [3].

Admittedly, implementation of modern views of learning in public schools is equally sketchy. David Lohman suggests three reasons for this slow progress despite enthusiastic acceptance by most professional educational organizations. (1) Many educators were well trained in methods based on behaviorism, particularly the theories of Skinner. Such well-entrenched beliefs are difficult to change, especially when the evidence that challenges the theory comes from texts, articles, and other printed materials. (2) Even teachers who were trained in recent years often have only the barest exposure to modern theories of thinking and development. (3) Those who have been trained thoroughly in modern instructional psychology soon find they must work in an educational system built on the foundation of behaviorism (Lohman, 1993).

Indeed, those of us who have taught for forty or more years will attest that many of the key features of the curriculum, classroom organizations, and student evaluation have not changed much since we were trained in the 1940s. Beliefs about the need for reinforcement, behavioral objectives, individualized instruction and objective tests are all rooted in the work of Edward Thorndyke and his "Law of Effect." In his view, memory consisted of a vast collection of specific responses to specific stimuli. Transfer depended on whether two situations shared the same stimuli elements. Broad transfer was an improbable goal using these concepts.

In cognitive theory, the organization of knowledge and transferability of skill are paramount. Most cognitive theories distinguish several different types of memory systems, different types of memory codes and different types of mental processes that operate on the learning task.

Many theorists distinguish between fact knowledge and skill knowledge. This basic dichotomy has several important implications for curriculum development and assessment. The Fundamentalist critics of OBE say they want a return to the basics and more rote learning. The problem is not the learning of facts, but the learning of thousands of disconnected facts:

In spite of frequent claims to the contrary by some educators, much of education consists of an attempt to impart factual knowledge to students. Research in cognitive psychology tells us that the single most important thing we need to know about a student's factual knowledge is how richly and flexibly the student has organized this knowledge. Such organizational schemes show that the learner has distinguished main ideas from less important ideas from details, and has related this new knowledge to old knowledge. . . .

Research also suggests that, contrary to much current educational practice, when learning factual knowledge, a good motto is "less can be more." Students in elementary biology are expected to learn thousands of technical, unfamiliar terms, to relate them to each other, and to apply this knowledge to problems in other domains. A thorough understanding of a smaller set of main ideas is much better than a vague and piecemeal understanding of a much larger set of ideas. (Lohman, 1993)

The spokespeople for the Fundamentalists who rail against the whole-language approach to reading and insist upon drills in phonics are clearly following behaviorist views from the past.

Learners usually achieve transfer only after much experience in applying newly acquired knowledge to an increasingly diverse array of problems. This means that teaching for transfer requires constant review within and between possible domains. Lohman argues that this is probably impossible to achieve unless teachers know what students are learning in other classes and content domains, and actively encourage them to discover relationships among domains. Compartmentalization of teaching leads to compartmentalization of knowledge. That has been what OBE experts have been saying all along.

CONCLUSIONS

Fundamentalists truly believe that they represent the majority of Americans and that they are doing God's work. Simonds has repeatedly said, "God is using us to save the children." William Bennett named his 1992 book *The Devaluing of America: The Fight for Our Children's Minds and Our Culture*. Removing prayer from the classroom and school functions has clearly been a major rallying point for religious conservatives. How can you say prayer is wrong but condoms are right? Clearly, the enemies of the Religious Right include multicultural curricula, performance-based education that stresses independent thinking, sex and AIDS education (except for the concept of abstinence), puppets that are used to teach children self-esteem, free breakfast programs for poor children (considered to weaken the family), and some books that the Right considers offensive.

The Free World Research Report (a conservative monthly that constantly attacks "government schools") listed eighteen key components of transformation that are to be considered taboo by state governments. The list includes almost everything that forward-looking school districts and states are trying to do. The authors of the list are unnamed, but they suggest that, "By publishing the list we hope to educate people across the country." Examples include tying teacher performance to pay, tying school accreditation to student performance, shared decision making, outcome-based assessment, pilot projects, facilitation technology, etc.

Each key component has a multitude of subideas. The outcome-based assessment items will illustrate the detailed flow of logic that the authors have included:

> 7. Outcomes-Based assessment tests. Look for buzzwords like thresholds, benchmarks, results-based rubrics, etc. Noteworthy because of absence of academics or inclusion of token amount of academics. Look for attitudes, character, values, social responsibility, service (community service) and other words descriptive of attitudes and feeling. ("When Outcomes . . .," 1993)

It is tempting to conclude that the Fundamentalists simply want to turn back the clock and "Christianize" the public schools. Certainly, that goal should concern anyone who cares about religious freedom. Their intermediate agenda is equally alarming. They are saying, "Let's water down the teaching of evolution, stop discussing sex, get rid of classes on self-esteem, and clear all of those bad books out of the library." Their prescriptions would make a mockery of effective teaching methods and curriculum renewal, perhaps the ultimate school improvement technique. Many of their positions are purely racist.

Clearly, the Right is wrong. The real challenge is how to stand up to them as educators and how to get parents—all parents—to stand up for their children's education. Presently, many public school districts are self-censoring to avoid the conflict. In the next chapter, I'll examine better ways to respond, starting with the values that substantial majorities of Americans would have the public schools teach.

ENDNOTES

1. Character development courses may be a bit of a reach without teaching values, which the Religious Right insists must not be done in OBE programs.
2. It's curious that the experts of the Religious Right always see OBE as antithetical to the basic skills. One wonders if they have ever read a state or local educational agency's plan.
3. Most leaders of the Religious Right get their information about the best ways to teach from memories of their own school days and from teachers and heads of independent schools. In twenty years of providing staff development for independent school faculties, I have always been struck by the almost perverse pride that private school folks take in the fact that they "have never taken one course in educational methods." That fact is coupled with an almost embarrassing curiosity about how research on teaching suggests they can get better results with their own students.

REFERENCES

Arocha, Z. 1993. "The Religious Right's March into Public School Government," *The School Administrator* (October):8–15.

Bracey, G. W. 1993. "George Will's Urban Legend," *Education Week* (September 29):29–30.

Gardner, H. 1987. *The Mind's New Science: A History of the Cognitive Revolution.* New York: Basic Books.

Harp, L. 1993. "Pa. Parent Becomes Mother of 'Outcomes' Revolt," *Education Week* (September 22):1.

Hughes, R. 1993. *Culture of Complaint: The Fraying of America.* Oxford: Oxford University Press.

Kelly, T. F. 1993. "Of Good and Evil and O.B.E.," *The Effective School Report* (September):1–2.

Leo-Nyquist, D. 1993. "The Crucial Role of Rural Teachers in the Educational Reform Movement," *Country Teacher* (Spring/Summer):1–4.

Lohman, D. F. 1993. "Learning and the Nature of Educational Measurement," *NASSP Bulletin* (October):41–53.

Malkin, M. 1993. "A Victory over the Edu-Zealots," *The Des Moines Register* (September 25):7A.

Phi Delta Kappa. 1993. *School Ratings Rise, Finances Biggest Problem.* Bloomington, IN: The Fraternity, pp. 1–4.

Reed, R. E., Jr. 1993. "The Agenda of the Religious Right: The Christian Coalition," *The School Administrator* (October):16–18.

Simonds, R. L. 1993. "Citizens for Excellence in Education," *The School Administrator* (October):19–22.

Thomas, J. F. 1992. "Parents' Group Battling over Schools' Soul," *The Wichita Eagle* (October):1A.

1993. "When Outcomes Become Results," *Free World Research Report* (March):12–13.

Will, G. 1993. "Public School Teachers Send Their Children to Private Schools," *The Des Moines Register* (August 26):10A.

Winkler, K. J. 1993. "Scholarship. Historians Acknowledge Need to Address Long-Neglected Topic of American Conservatism," *The Chronicle of Higher Education* (April 28):A6–A13.

CHAPTER 4
Seeking a Middle Ground for School Reform

IS there a possibility of compromise? The issues include values to teach, Outcome-Based Education, Goals 2000, parental rights, school and societal violence, AIDS protection, local control, standards and assessment-driven school reform, globalism and multiculturalism, prayer in public schools, and programs that stress independent thinking and self-esteem.

Basic to understanding the seriousness of the struggle is the knowledge that American public education is not working for many of our children. It especially doesn't work in the big cities. Public education is a changing landscape. We have entered an era where the school curriculum is expanding (for example, what is taught today in junior high was often taught in high school ten years ago). Yet the time to provide instruction is declining. For the most part, the organization of America's school districts has not changed to reflect current national demographics. America is no longer a rural nation, but the majority of its school districts are located in very small towns and rural areas. Of our 15,500 school districts, 4000 of them have under 300 pupils; 6000 have fewer than 600 students. These are also the enrollment sizes of the typical independent school.

America is also strapped for cash. In the decennial study of the American public school superintendent, the American Association of School Administrators (1992) discovered that financing our schools was again the number one challenge for superintendents. However, collective bargaining was not in second place, as usual. Assessment and testing, accountability/credibility, and changing priorities in curriculum all vied for second place.

A quick glance at the educational headlines of the last three months of 1993 shows that the school reformers are making some progress, but it is on an uneven front. Perhaps some of the progress has come because of the defeat of the voucher plan in California and because the need to plan for the next presidential campaign has occupied William Bennett, Dan Quayle, Lamar Alexander, and Pat Buchanan.

In October 1993, Phi Delta Kappa and the Gallup organization released a poll showing that three-quarters of the public opposes sending children to private schools at public expense. At the same time, Governor John Engler proposed a radical solution to the states' self-imposed school finance crisis under which the state would provide grants to students to use to attend any public school.

On election day in California, school-choice advocates were dismayed by a two-to-one defeat of the ballot initiative calling for a statewide system of public and private school vouchers. A November report on Vermont's pioneering portfolio-based assessment program found that serious problems remain in the way that students are assessed in writing. A ruling by the United States Supreme Court made it easier for parents of children with disabilities to win public reimbursement for the costs of private schooling. At almost the same time, the American Federation of Teachers (AFT) decided to ask for a nationwide moratorium on inclusion programs for special education students.

December was a whirlwind of activities to tie up loose ends at the state and national level. A report by a federal advising committee finds scant evidence that money the federal government spends on mathematics and science education is leading to improvements in learning. New Jersey's previous governor Jim Florio (D) vetoed legislation that would require school districts to teach abstinence as the only way to avoid pregnancy and sexually transmitted disease. A New York appellate court ruled against New York City's condom-on-demand high school program. The court reasoned that parents' rights were violated due to the lack of a parental consent provision.

Parents from wealthy Connecticut schools joined forces with Fundamentalists to oppose that state's movement toward

Outcome-Based Education. The state plan has a familiar OBE look.

> Several components of the plan include granting a H.S. diploma, based not on the number of credits earned, but on students demonstrating they learned a set of skills; requiring schools to meet the educational needs of all students, including the gifted and disabled students; reorganizing schools to put more decision-making authority in the hands of principals and teachers; and eschewing letter grades for real learning. ("Outcomes-Based . . .," 1994, p. 3)

The comments had a familiar ring, too. In support, Frank Newman, President of the Education Commission of the States, said, "What is so striking is their opposition to something that is led by all of the relevant forces in the country when there is such a widespread sense that we need to do something about education in the United States." The suburban opposition answers, "This proposal will unnecessarily disturb and drag down our schools!" "There is a problem, but it's in the cities," said Kathleen Renton, a Greenwich PTA Council vice president. "Why do you have to apply the solution universally, where it is not needed?" Kay Wall, another Greenwich PTA member, criticized OBE by saying, "It's not a program that improves education; it's a program that rounds out education with all sorts of social goals." She and other Connecticut critics are concerned that Outcome-Based Education could "dumb down the curriculum."

Perhaps the funniest attack from the evangelicals was that of radio evangelist Rev. Joseph Chambers, who claimed that Barney the Dinosaur was a new age demon. Proclaiming that America is under siege from the powers of darkness, Chambers said in a pre-Christmas broadcast that "Barney is teaching kids that we must accept everyone as they are—whether they are homosexuals or lesbians" ("Barney a . . .," 1993).

THE REFORMS

Educational and political leaders and much of the general public want K–12 education to provide students with a better education, in part so that they may compete with the best students from Asia and Europe. This is often called "World-Class Education." Reformers also want to reduce violence in schools, avoid teenage pregnancies, stop substance abuse, and help America succeed as one of the most ethnically diverse nations of the world. No one can deny that these are lofty and desirable goals.

Patricia A. Graham, President of the Spencer Foundation, succinctly stated the challenge for the reformers: "For the last 150 years, we've held the pedagogy constant and let the results vary; in the future, we've got to vary the pedagogy and have high standards of accomplishment for all" ("What's In and Out in 1993," 1993, p. 43).

Education Week developed a "factoid" box based on what is wrong with American education and what needs to be done to fix it (Figure 4.1). To change the paradigm of public education that much, while also celebrating diversity via multiculturalism and

OUT	IN
Inputs	Outputs
Innate Ability	Effort
Rote Learning	Mastery
Autocratic	Autonomous
Seat Time	Accomplishment
Student as Learner	Student as Worker
Teacher as Lecturer	Teacher as Manager of Instruction
Longevity	Competence
Administrator as Master	Administrator as Servant
Centralized Bureaucracy	Decentralized Management
Technology: Bells and Whistles	Technology: Productivity Enhancer
School Board: Micro management	School Trustees: Stewardship
Time: Periods, Semesters, Years	Time: Flexible
Schools: Teacher Proof	Schools: Teacher Friendly
Diploma = Seat Time	Diploma = Mastery
Age	Accomplishment
Superintendent = Dictator	Superintendent = Choreographer
Taxpayer	Shareholder
Standardization	Standards
True and False Tests	Authentic Assessment
Blue Collar	Professionals
Uniform Salary Schedule	Pay for Scarcity; Pay for Performance
Education: School's Business	Education: Everyone's Business
School = Building	School = Learning

FIGURE 4.1 *What's in and what's out in 1993 (source:* Education Week, *January 13, 1993, p. 43).*

global education, is bound to be a tall order. At the national level, the vehicle of choice is Goals 2000. States, while working toward Goals 2000 through the Governors' Conference, have flirted with various versions of Outcome-Based Education. Local public school agencies have embraced both but generally find that a truly revised curriculum and assessment plan is beyond their resources. Interestingly, independent schools have taken the new mathematics and science standards seriously, at least at the upper school level (Commission on Standards for School Mathematics, 1989; National Committee on Science Education Standards and Assessment, 1993).

THE GOALS

Inspired by then President George Bush and the nation's governors during their "Education Summit" in 1989, the 1991 National Education Goals Panel report, *Building a Nation of Learners*, is lofty and crucial, albeit somewhat lacking in focus and substance (Young, 1993a). The National Education Goals Panel monitors progress toward Goals 2000. Undergirding the goals, the National Education Standards Improvement Council (NESIC) develops criteria for content standards and works with the states to certify their assessments.

For several reasons, including opposition by critics of outcomes and standards and teaching values, this work is progressing slowly. In less than seven years, Goals 2000 will enter the twenty-first century. Judging from the progress checks made by the National Education Goals Panel, America won't make it! Nebraska Governor E. Benjamin Nelson, outgoing chair of the Goals Panel, said "Despite moderate gains, our progress is wholly inadequate if we hope to meet the national educational goals by the year 2000."

Goals one and two deal with "starting school ready to learn" and a "90 percent graduation rate"; goals five and six center on "literate adults" and "drug- and violence-free schools." The argument between the Fundamentalists and the public schools targets goals three and four.

Goal three: by the year 2000, American students will leave grades four, eight, and twelve having demonstrated competency in challenging subject matter, including English, mathematics, science, history, and geography, and every school in America will ensure that all students learn to use their minds well, so they may be prepared for responsible citizenship, further learning, and productive employment in our modern economy.

Goal four: by the year 2000, United States students will be first in the world in science and mathematics achievement.

The third report on the national goals, released in Washington D.C. on September 30, 1993, concludes that "at no stage in a learner's life—before formal schooling, during the school years, or as adults—are Americans doing as well as they should or can." In regard to the third and fourth goals, the Goals Panel reports:

> Goal Three: U.S. students will leave grades four, eight, and twelve competent in challenging subject matter and prepared for responsible citizenship, lifelong learning and productive employment.
>
> No more than a quarter of students in grades four, eight, and twelve can master challenging math. Roughly a third meet the Goals Panel performance standard in reading. Only half of 12th graders understand how government works.
>
> Goal Four: U.S. students will be first in the world in science and mathematics achievement.
>
> U.S. students score consistently lower than students from other countries in international science and math assessments. Only 17 percent of fourth graders regularly use calculators for math and only 44 percent have access to computers. For eighth graders, the numbers are 56 percent and 20 percent. (Young, 1993b, p. 6)

Goal three is an educational goal clearly in the control of schools. This goal pays attention to time (grades four, eight, and twelve) and defines curriculum areas that must pass muster. Goal four has the clear purpose of developing science and mathematics content and performance standards that match or surpass those in other developed countries.

Setting aside the logistical nightmare of making the international comparisons required by goal four and the continuing fight over what national standards and national assessment means, much can be done by a local school to specify curriculum content, to sequence instructional delivery, and to create assessment that accurately portrays student achievement progress. Systematic data collection will provide credible information.

Presently, little attention is paid to making the goals/standards/assessment model work through the attainment of curriculum alignment. Goals 2000 is viewed as a lighthouse of "high standards" that will guide states and local schools. Goals alone, however, won't assure that higher standards occur. Curriculum alignment means that the written curriculum, the taught curriculum, and the tested curriculum, are all the same. Goals 2000 addresses the written (or planned curriculum) but, so far, only in very general and unmeasurable terms. Goals 2000 also calls for assessment (grades four, eight, and twelve at the least; annually if "report cards" of achievement at the local, state, and national levels continue). What is missing is the infusion of the goals into the "taught curriculum."

In December of 1993, the five former United States Secretaries of Education met to discuss standards (Pisch, 1994). All agreed that it is important to hold students to high standards. They had no agreement, however, on who should set the standards, how students should be evaluated, whether money should be tied to the imposition and achievement of standards, and what the proper role of the federal government is.

Richard W. Riley, the current Secretary of Education, was on a nationwide tour during March and April of 1994. His stated purpose was to promote understanding of Goals 2000 and President Clinton's first education bill, the Goals 2000: Educate America Act. He calls Goals 2000 a great first step as the mechanism for establishing world-class content and performance standards (see Figure 4.2). In Riley's view, those goals are bipartisan because all fifty governors and President Bush collaboratively set them in 1989. He intends to use the goals as part of a national commitment to develop where we want to go in education, or "what our young people should know at various levels and what they should be able to do" (Young, 1993b). "Next, we should tie that process into the state's work. Each of the fifty states should develop its own systematic reform plan, similar to the voluntary national standards, but designed to match the states' own needs and circumstances."

1. By the year 2000, all children in America will start school ready to learn.

2. By the year 2000, the high school graduation rate will increase to at least 90 percent.

3. By the year 2000, American students will leave grades four, eight, and twelve having demonstrated competency in challenging subject matter, including English, mathematics, science, history, and geography; and every school in America will ensure that all students learn to use their minds well, so they may be prepared for responsible citizenship, further learning, and productive employment in our modern economy.

4. By the year 2000, U.S. students will be first in the world in science and mathematics achievement.

5. By the year 2000, every adult American will be literate and will possess the knowledge and skills necessary to compete in a global economy and exercise the rights and responsibilities of citizenship.

6. By the year 2000, every school in America will be free of drugs and violence and will offer a disciplined environment conducive to learning.

FIGURE 4.2 Goals 2000 (source: National Education Goals Panel Report, Building a Nation of Learners).

Mr. Riley's predecessors as Secretary of Education were not sure that goals/standards/assessment was the road to world-class education; Lauro Cavazos, Lamar Alexander, and William J. Bennett were opposed to standards for various reasons. Terrel H. Bell and Shirley M. Hufstedler were more supportive of voluntary standards [1].

"I have great reservations about national standards, frankly," said Cavazos. "I think that once you establish a standard—although it's voluntary and we can change it and people do not have to accept it—I have seen too many volunteer things started out in Washington that subsequently became law."

Lamar Alexander praised the standard-setting efforts underway in various disciplines, most of which were started on his watch during the Bush administration, but he questioned the wisdom of tying federal dollars to the so-called "school delivery standards" that are to measure the conditions needed in schools to allow students to meet academic standards.

If the Clinton education bill (Goals 2000: Educate America Act) passes in its present form, each state would have to set such standards in order to receive education-reform funds. Using Atlanta as an example, Alexander said, "None of us when we are in Washington are wise enough to say how a district ought to spend its money and what it ought to spend in order to help children here learn to live, work, and compete in the world they live in today."

William J. Bennett, always the most "quotable" Education Secretary, said he wanted to keep educational reform simple when he wrote the chapter "What Works in American Education, and Why":

> There is probably no field in which the statement of the obvious, of simple truths, is more necessary than in education. It is the bias of the intellectual to value the complex over the simple. The important thing to keep in mind about American education is that *we know what works*. Education reform is not an arcane business; it is not primarily a matter of great complexity, but one of will and political courage. It involves the willingness to hold institutions and individuals accountable, to make a commitment to each child, and the courage when necessary to challenge and change the system. (Bennett, 1992, p. 71)

Bennett claims that the imposition of academically rigorous national tests would make more sense [2]. Standards will never be imposed, according to Bennett, because conservatives fear that they will lead to a Congressionally imposed curriculum, while liberals fear that some groups will not be able to reach such standards.

Bennett closed with one of his trademark sound bites, "There is this worry throughout liberal circles; therefore, we will not have a standard; we'll have several circles. We'll have a trying-hard standard, a self-esteem standard and a how-do-you-feel-about-things standard."

Testing establishes benchmarks for students, schools, and districts, he said, and provides incentives for students to do well.

Bell, who will be remembered for the controversial "wall chart" comparing states on several academic indicators and for the landmark report, *A Nation at Risk,* said that "there is a yearning for a means of measurement." All of the secretaries seem to forget that all of the projects charged with setting national curriculum goals and standards are also recommending means of assessment!

Finally, Hufstedler and Bennett, in a rare moment of agreement, said that the United States is spending an adequate amount on education, but Hufstedler added that incentives are needed for students to meet high standards and suggested that federal dollars are a good incentive: "I think the concept of reward and incentive is just as important in spending federal funds as it is in spending private funds." Interestingly, this is a theme that has been woven through several guidelines for FIRST grant applications since Riley has been Education Secretary [3].

Regardless of the final form of the Clinton education bill, numerous groups were hard at work setting goals and standards. The directors of the projects charged with setting the national standards are exploring how—and whether—some of the emerging standards should be integrated, especially for students in primary grades. Because students naturally learn in integrative ways (although teachers may not teach that way), some critics contend that setting separate subject-matter standards creates artificial boundaries among subjects and inhibits interdisciplinary learning.

The goals' authors also realize that subjects are usually taught in broad themes at the K–3 level. The fear is that putting too much on a teacher's desk, discipline by discipline, would be intimidating.

During 1993, the Department of Education was funding standards projects in eight areas: the arts, civics, English, foreign language, geography, history, mathematics, and science. The National Council for Social Studies and the National Council on Economic Education are working on their own to set standards in their disciplines (Viandro, 1993a).

WORLD-CLASS SCHOOLS

What do we mean when we say America needs world-class schools? "The term gets tossed around so much that nobody understands what it means," says Professor Donald A. Chalker, chair of the department of administration, curriculum, and instruction at Western Carolina University. Chalker and Professor Richard Haynes at the same university are co-authors of a new study comparing the public education systems of the United States, Canada, France, Germany, Britain, New Zealand, Taiwan, Israel, Japan, and South Korea. The nations were selected because of the strong reputations of their public schools and because American students fare poorly in mathematics and science comparisons with them (Viandro, 1993b).

Chalker and Haynes admit that they did not control for the greater socioeconomic, academic, and ethnic diversity among American students. For that reason, the United States may well have to spend more than other nations on education. Nonetheless, even a casual examination of their results, summarized in Figure 4.3, reveals that the biggest differences (the World Classness) are cultural. Chalker says his big conclusion is that "we have the schools we want to have. People in this country do not want a longer school year or to limit TV watching."

Other nations expect education to be hard work; Americans

World – Class Standards		How the U.S. Compares
INPUTS		
Average class size	+	smaller
Amount of teacher preparation	+	more
Spending for education:		
per student basis	+	more
percent of GNP	+	more
Course offerings	0	same
Time spent in school	-	less
Amount of homework	-	less
Length of school year	-	less
CULTURAL SUPPORT		
Respect for teachers	-	less
Watching Recreational TV	-	more
Academic Pressure	-	less
Education is a serious enterprise (hard work)	-	No, education is "fun"
Academic pressure causes teen suicides	-	much higher in U.S. 15-24 year olds

FIGURE 4.3 World-class school differences—U.S. and the competition (source: Chalker and Haynes, World Class Schools, 1994, Lancaster, PA: Technomic Publishing Co., Inc.).

view learning as *fun*. When Taiwanese children, for example, are chosen to participate in the International Assessment of Educational Progress, they stand at attention when their names are called and then march proudly out of the classroom to the applause of their classmates. To them it's a matter of patriotism and national pride—to American kids its just another damn bubble sheet.

Chalker notes that when Japanese children are sick, for example, their mother attends school for them and takes notes. Four out of five American mothers would be working and hoping that *this time* the husband would call in sick to stay home with the child. While American kindergartens are viewed as socializing experiences, French kindergartners are taught basic academic skills from the start.

The two researchers also put to rest the persistent myth that other nations put great pressure on kids to excel academically and that it leads to higher suicide rates. The study shows that the suicide rates of young people, fifteen to twenty-four years old, in the United States are among the highest in the world.

OUTCOME-BASED EDUCATION

In Chapter 2, I introduced OBE by saying

> Alarmed by the growing number of high school graduates who can't cope with life in the real world, state and local educational leaders are shifting the focus from how much time is spent in the classroom to what graduates actually know. The methodology for this shift in emphasis is called Outcome-Based Education, the brainchild of educational consultant William Spady, which sets specific achievement levels students must reach in each subject before graduation.

OBE has been stopped cold in some states (Iowa is one), stalled for a while in others (Pennsylvania), and is in contention in still others, e.g., Colorado, Wyoming and Connecticut.

William Spady is not known as a researcher—he is a guru. As such, he has a considerable following, including much of the United States business community. His ideas are spellbinding, at least the first time you hear his *very* routinized pitch. (It grows a bit thin through the second, third, and fourth time.) His ideas come from the heart—and from Bloom, Block, and Hunter. His model is contained in two pages (Figure 4.4, p. 95)—much of what he says are popular slogans from the school reform movement of the late 1970s, viz., "All students can learn," "Success breeds success," and "Schools control the conditions of success."

His principles are used to set graduation outcomes and to guide curriculum planning. Unfortunately, they are so sweeping and so loose that all kinds of local filigree is added as districts and states work toward the OBE future.

The Connecticut plan for school reform was presented to the legislature by a panel that promised an "outcome-based, world class educational system."

Several components of the plan include granting a H.S. diploma based not on the number of credits earned, but on students demonstrating they learned a set of skills; requiring schools to meet the educational needs of all students, including the gifted and disabled students; reorganizing schools to put more decision-making authority in the hands of principals and teachers; and eschewing letter grades for real learning.

In Connecticut, the plan met its greatest resistance in upper middle-class Greenwich. In Wyoming, OBE drew fire in the trendy vacation spot of Jackson.

> Following a state mandate, ninth graders in the Jackson Hole High School will be required to meet new, controversial performance standards when they graduate in 1997.
>
> The debate dividing the community is focused on what those standards should be and how they will be implemented. For two years, the Teton County School District has been attempting to meet the state's charge by developing an Outcome Based Education plan that the public has scrutinized and criticized.
>
> For many people, the issue is muddled in educational jargon. In an OBE system, students will study traditional subjects but may not be graded in a traditional manner. Instead, they will be asked to demonstrate meaningful knowledge and skills in all subject areas. Testing will still include exams, but portfolios, projects and group work will also be considered when a student is evaluated.
>
> For Superintendent Tom Nelson, the idea of making students accountable to community prescribed standards is clear. "We're going to set some thresholds that we want students to meet," he said.

OUTCOME-BASED EDUCATION

Four Operational Principles
- Principles 1: Clarity of Focus
- Principles 2: Expanded Opportunity and Instructional Support
- Principles 3: High Expectations for Learning Success
- Principle 4: Design Down From Your Ultimate Outcomes

The "Success for All" Approach Rests on These Tenets:
1. All students can learn
2. Success breeds success
3. Schools control the condition of success

Defining Learner Outcomes at All Levels Must Answer Three Questions:
1. What should students know? (knowledge)
2. What should students be able to do? (skills)
3. What should students feel and believe? (values and attitudes, work ethic, work together cooperatively, etc.)

OBE Focuses On Student Outcomes
MASTERY LEARNING

Mastery Learning has been traditionally defined as both a philosophy of school learning and an associated set of specific instructional practices. The philosophical premise of Master learning is that **all children can learn** when provided with conditions that are appropriate for their learning.

Two Essential Elements Form the Basics of Mastery Learning.
1. Corrective and enrichment feedback must be provided on a *regular* and *specific* manner.
2. Congruence between the instruction components of curriculum, instruction and assessment, must exist.

Mastery Learning Focuses On Student Mastery Of Material
MASTERY TEACHING

Mastery teaching is a decision-making model that translates established principles from educational psychology into procedures teachers should follow to assure that their students learn well.

Mastery Teaching Elements
1. Anticipatory set
2. Statement of objectives
3. Input and modeling
4. Guided practice
5. Independent practice
6. Closure
7. Assessment

Mastery Teaching focuses On Teacher Behaviors

FIGURE 4.4 Outcome-Based Education (source: William Spady's workshop, Introduction to OBE).

"It will no longer be acceptable for students to skate through with D's and F's." (Dewell, 1993, p. 1)

Tim Westerberg is a disciple of Bill Spady. He is also a very skilled administrator trained here at Iowa State University. He planned to graduate the first OBE high school class in the nation with the class of 1994–1995. Unfortunately, his school, Littleton (CO) High School, got blindsided by three new board members who, while denying they have formal ties to Religious Right groups, are determined to restore "traditional education" to Littleton. The restoration may not be pleasant.

> Once this was a sedate suburb where the problem most likely to provoke anger was a snarled commute after a busy day at the office. No longer. Last week, a Littleton school board meeting became so heated the sheriff was called. And that wasn't an isolated incident. As many as 400 people now turn out for meetings that used to draw sleepy crowds of fewer than 39.
>
> The difference can be traced to the five-member school board, whose three new members have vowed to restore "traditional education" to Littleton. Unlike many back-to-basics efforts across the country, board members in Littleton claim no formal ties to religious right groups. But they are meeting fierce resistance from supporters of reforms that were under way when the newcomers took office.
>
> Since November, the two sides have clashed on everything from where Superintendent Cile Chavez should sit during board meetings to whether to approve a proclamation in support of Education Week. (Bingham, 1993)

How OBE Works

Outcome-Based Education is a goals-setting, curriculum-building process. It has no curriculum content; instead, it is a recipe for a local educational agency or state to plan a new curriculum content for K–12 subjects (or integrated subjects). A committee or a task force is named to think through the most fundamental questions in education, viz., what should students (at the end of the K–12 years) know and be able to do? And how should they demonstrate that knowledge?

The goals group often talks for months (or years!) about these questions. When their work is completed, the group typically recommends ten to twenty-five "requirements" [4]. Teton County Schools (Jackson, WY) have twelve (Figure 4.5). For example, at Littleton High School, seniors must prove they can use a foreign language by writing a letter via that language to a friend. They assemble writing portfolios representing academics essays, fictional narrative and poetry, journalistic or business writing, and personal communication. Scoring sheets called "rubrics" describe "excellent," "proficient," and "unacceptable" levels of performance (see Figures 4.6 and 4.7 for a contrast of the new and old assessment methods at Littleton).

A letter in French or a speech before a public body are fairly concrete. Goals committees also believe that learning outcomes should contain values as well as concepts and skills. At Little-

---

Current graduation requirements
- 4 English units, 3 math units, 3 science units, 3 social studies units, 1 vocational unit, 1 physical education unit, 1 humanities unit, $1/2$ unit of health, 9 units of electives
- 25 total units required for graduation with at least a D in each of those 24 units
- A unit is a year-long class

Exit outcomes for a graduate of Teton County Schools
(To be in place by 1997)

Essential skills
- Communication: reading writing, speaking, listening
- Mathematics and science concepts and processes
- Technology awareness and use

Creative and reasoning skills
- Problem solving
- Investigation and research
- Creative expression

Responsible citizenship
- Cooperation and group work
- Diversity
- Stewardship and service
- Historical knowledge and civic responsibility
- Responsible decision making
- Positive attitude and work ethic

FIGURE 4.5 Conventional and OBE graduation requirements, Teton County Schools, Jackson, Wyoming (source: Jackson Hole News, December 8, 1993).

COMMUNICATION I: DEMONSTRATION 4--
SPEAKING PERSUASIVE SPEAKING RUBRIC

Presentation is characterized by:	EXCELLENT	PROFICIENT	UNACCEPTABLE	COMMENTS
DELIVERY:				
Visual Presentation	• Body language projects nonverbal poise controlled use of space, and effective use of audio/visual technologies when used.	• Erect posture, relaxed facial expression, natural use of gestures, effective us of visual aids when appropriate, acceptable use of podium and of movement. eye contact and energy appropriate.	• Appearance of gestures not appropriate, lacks eye contact or reads speech	
Vocal Presentation	• Sounds enthusiastic, assertive. Articulation and pronunciation are clear	• Includes conversational tone, control of vocal pauses, rate, pitch, and loudness. Articulation and pronunciation are acceptable*	• Giggling, expounding, or other vocal behaviors which interfere with transfer of message; speaks too fast or too slow; runs words together, pronunciation interferes with message.	
Word Choice	• Enhances the purpose or adjusts to audience reactions	• Grammar is correct (i.e., subject/verb agreement, pronoun/antecedent agreement.)	• Word choice is characterized by inappropriate language, cliches, language, vernacular, double negatives, sexist.	

FIGURE 4.6 Scoring rubric for communication demonstration, Littleton (CO) Public Schools (source: The Sunday Denver Post, December 12, 1993).

ORGANIZATION	EXCELLENT	PROFICIENT	UNACCEPTABLE	COMMENTS
Introduction	• Clear, prepared • Uses humor, dramatic tension, or analogy as a key element without detracting from the integrity of the content.	• Introduction, body and conclusion. • Uses introductory attention device, clearly states thesis, previews main points.	• Unclear intention, is not prepared. • Lacks attention-getting device, unclear or missing thesis statement.	
Body	• Advocates a course of action, explains why the course of action is important, presents a two-sided message.	• Advocates a general course of action.	• Course of action is not realistic or no course of action is suggested.	
Conclusion	• Uses concluding techniques, such as mirroring, application, or reinforcement.	• Uses concluding technique (i.e., repetition for effect.)	• Ends without appropriate conclusion.	
CONTENT:				
etc.				

FIGURE 4.6 (continued) Scoring rubric for communication demonstration, Littleton (CO) Public Schools (*source:* The Sunday Denver Post, December 12, 1993).

> **FINAL EXAMINATION**
> **FUNDAMENTALS OF SPEECH**
>
> TRUE/FALSE QUESTIONS:
>
> On the answer sheet, write out the word TRUE or FALSE to indicate your response to the following statements. Each answer on this test is worth 2 points. The essay points are indicated by the question.
>
> ____ 1. The impression of a speaker's credibility will determine how persuasive that person can be.
>
> ____ 2. Assuming that neither party objects, the closer the distance between people, the more comfortable or intimate is their relationship.
>
> ____ 3. It is acceptable to present a hypothetical illustration as fact to enhance its impact.
>
> ____ 4. Besides aiding in preparation and delivery, a specific purpose gives the listener a frame of reference in which to place the speaker's remarks and so should be presented first in the introduction.
>
> ____ 5. The impromptu speech has been researched, practiced, and outlined before presentation.
>
> ____ 6. Aristotle observed that there are three instruments of persuasion: argument, emotion, and character.
>
> *etc.*

FIGURE 4.7. *Traditional testing format for Communications I course, Littleton (CO) Public Schools (source:* The Sunday Denver Post, *December 12, 1993).*

ton, one of the requirements states that graduates must show that they "interact well and work cooperatively with others." The rubric calls for rating whether they are "able to compromise personal position when appropriate." Not surprisingly, critics say there is no way to measure when to compromise: "Each person has to make that decision for himself—there are no standards."

After the goals or outcomes are specified, Spady's approach to OBE uses principle four: "Design down from your ultimate outcomes." This means that, after a goals committee describes what a graduate should know, be, and do, the faculty must plan and write strands of learning, learner outcomes, and a scope and sequence to follow. This is known as "planning up." This is also very hard, highly intellectual work that requires many hours of faculty effort in K–12 groups, for each subject. (Spady would probably say no subjects are needed.)

Writing new forms of assessment is much more appealing and has a cachet of being on the cutting edge. Terms such as *nontra-*

ditional assessment, authentic assessment, and *the three P's* (Portfolio, Performance, and Product) are used. Unfortunately, the new assessments and new ways of reporting student progress to parents often take precedence over the necessary two or three years of curriculum renewal and alignment.

Even more troubling, at least to critics of OBE, is that those who propose OBE also begin to talk about mastery learning—but they don't talk with the depth of understanding that Bloom or Block might provide. Instead, they use slogans such as "all children can learn—when provided with conditions that are appropriate for their learning," "Success breeds success," and "Schools control the conditions of success." They say that an essential element of mastery learning is that "corrective and enrichment feedback must be provided in a *regular* and *scientific* manner."

Peter Overly, a parent in Jackson, Wyoming, wonders how the schools are going to be able to keep students from falling through the cracks without watering down the curriculum: "I don't think expectations are very high now and I'd hate to see them lowered. From what I understand about OBE, everyone must meet certain outcomes, which implies to me that equal opportunity to learn is not enough. Now we have to guarantee equal outcomes" (Dewell, 1993, p. 1).

The OBE logic includes getting rid of letter grades, Carnegie Units, and graduation based on accumulation of seat time, i.e., graduating when a student has served enough time (Figure 4.8).

Critics of OBE also fear that too much emphasis is placed on skills and not enough on content. They want assurances that students understand not only the process of historical research and analysis, but the basic facts about events such as the Depression and the Holocaust. Critics of all stripes, not just conservatives and evangelicals, point out that OBE has no research, not even case studies of the process, being used successfully. They argue that Johnson City, New York, schools mainly changed teaching method (to mastery teaching) but never developed an OBE curriculum or moved to high-stakes testing of performance demonstrations in order to graduate.

Even ardent foes such as Phyllis Schlafly have admitted that "outcome-based education is sweeping the country in the name of

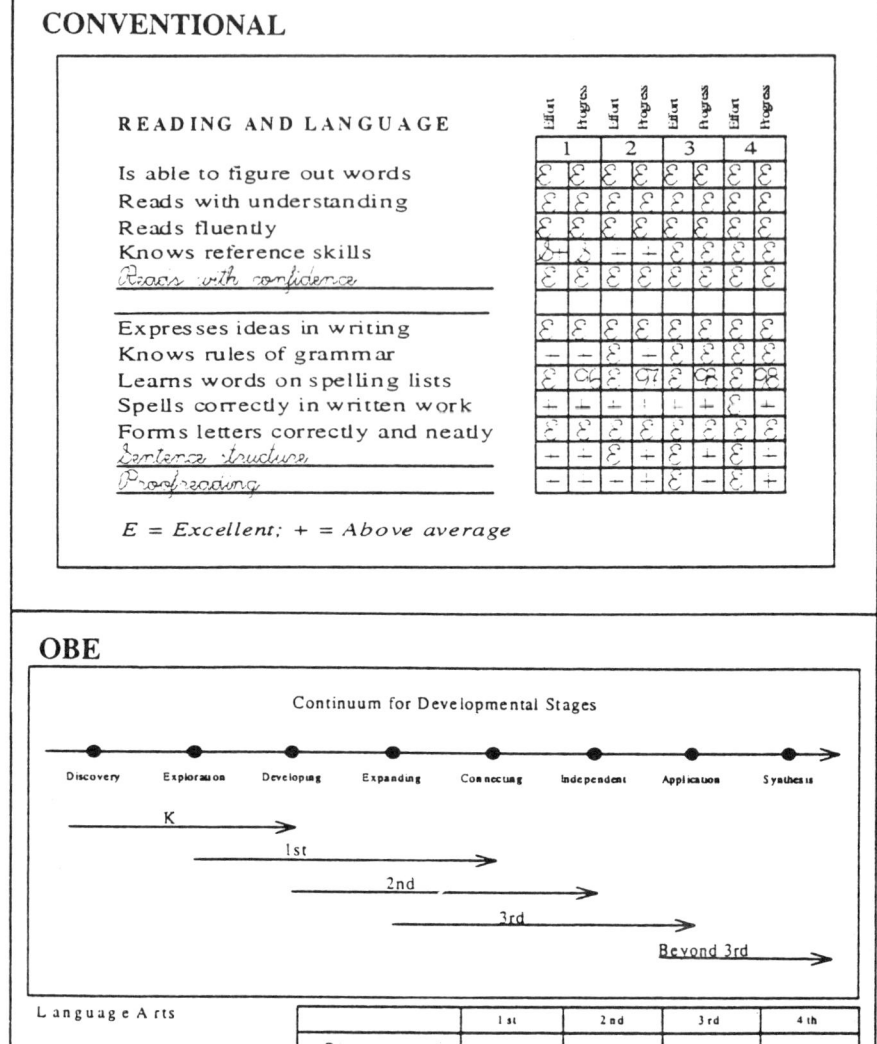

FIGURE 4.8 *A comparison of a conventional report card and an OBE progress report (source:* Jackson Hole News, *December 8, 1993).*

school 'restructuring.' Since the American people seem ready to accept drastic surgery on our failed public schools, state departments of education are seizing this opportunity to force acceptance of OBE as the cure" (Schlafly, 1993, p. 20). C. J. Varnum and Richard L. King, writing in the spring 1993 issue of *Outcomes*, called OBE in the United States "a tidal wave of change" (Varnum and King, 1993). In their nationwide telephone survey of all fifty states, they claim that forty-two were pursuing OBE at the state level "as the most promising strategy for improving education for all students."

OPPOSITION TO SCHOOL CHANGE

Paul Cummins, president of Crossroads Community Foundation, a group dedicated to helping restore local public schools' arts programs, cuts to the heart of the matter: "Public schools have become the dumping grounds for all the social and economic problems we have not been willing to deal with as a nation. The challenge here in Los Angeles is, will the wealthy enclaves just sort of wall themselves off, and will the city disintegrate into groups that are hostile and unequal?" (Sommerfield, 1993b).

The Fundamentalist membership is generally composed of middle-class whites. They tolerate the way schools are—especially if their children or grandchildren are not in *public schools*. Female members of this group tend to be among the one out of five mothers in the United States who stays home during the child-rearing years. In eighteen months of sifting through what is happening in the school wars, I have found no instance where the Religious Right has come forward with any program for change for the public schools. They want things the way they are—or vouchers to enable their children to escape to a "better" private education.

Phyllis Schlafly summarizes all the opposition to OBE in ten major objections that she claims parents have raised against OBE. She writes that OBE is a process for telling our children how to live, what to say, what to think, what to know, and what not to know. "OBE is converting the three R's to the three D's: Deliberately Dumbed Down."

Here are Schlafly's (1993) ten objections:

1. OBE is packaged in a deceptive language that appears to be mischievously chosen to mislead parents.
2. OBE uses students as guinea pigs in a vast social experiment. OBE advocates are not able to produce any replicable research or pilot studies to show that it works.
3. OBE offers no method of accountability to students, parents, teachers, or taxpayers.
4. OBE is a dumbed-down, egalitarian scheme that stifles individual potential for excellence and achievement by holding the entire class to the level of learning attainable by every child.
5. In an OBE system, academic and factual subject matter is replaced by vague and subjective learning outcomes.
6. A high percentage of OBE "outcomes" concern values, attitudes, opinions, and relationships rather than objective information.
7. OBE sets up a computer file on each child to track the child's efforts to master the learning outcomes. These "electronic portfolios" will take the place of traditional assessments and test results and will become the basis for the school's efforts to remediate whatever attitudes and behaviors the school deems unacceptable.
8. OBE is a method for concealing and perpetuating the number one crime of the public school system—the failure to teach first graders how to read. OBE is wholly committed to the "whole-language," word-guessing method, rather than the phonics method. This ensures that children will learn only to memorize a few words that are massively repeated. Teachers are cautioned not to correct spelling and syntax errors because that could be damaging to the student's self-esteem and creativity.
9. OBE, of course, involves high costs for administration and the retraining of teachers in an entirely new system, which

will be reflected in higher school taxes. The computer portfolio system is reported to be five times as expensive as traditional assessment tests. Putting computers into the hands of first-graders to give the facade of moving into modern technology is a gross waste of funds. Computers may actually be a detriment to learning elementary writing and arithmetic skills, but they may be very useful in changing values, as noted above.

10. OBE involves tightened state control at the expense of local control. Although OBE salespersons claim otherwise, the new system tightens the grip of state education officials and federal education laboratories because they write the required outcomes, develop the curriculum, train the teachers, and judge the performance of the students (all of whom must conform to national goals).

Even when private funds are used to reform public schools, the opposition forms. School officials in Gastonia, North Carolina, were delighted to win the competition for one of the New American School Development Corporation awards to be one of the new "break the mold" public schools. Now they are under fire from hundreds of local conservative Christian activists who are questioning the project's academic integrity and saying it would undermine their children's religious beliefs.

> Educators in Gaston County, a blue-collar, textile-manufacturing region outside Charlotte, had high hopes that the $2.1 million they received from the New American Schools Development Corporation for the first year of a five-year project would revolutionize county schools.
>
> Their Odyssey Project was one of 11 proposals selected to receive a grant from the private, nonprofit corporation created at the behest of former President Bush to raise $200 million to create innovative schools.
>
> The project plans to abandon traditional grade levels, introduce older students to weekly seminars on multiculturalism and current events, require community service of all students, and use an outcome-based assessment that focuses not on the number of courses taken, but on the knowledge, skills, and attitudes students must have before graduation.

Ironically, while one of the project's primary goals is to enhance parental and community involvement, the unprecedented involvement of some community members now poses a challenge to its implementation.

Leaders of Concerned Citizens for Public Education, an organization formed to fight the project, have a long list of objections, but most of their ire is directed toward its outcome-based approach—often a target of conservatives, who say it forces schools to teach values at the expense of core subjects. (Sommerfield, 1993a)

The project has even come under fire for its use of Greek terms, which one opponent decried because the ancient Greeks practiced sodomy. One project planner heard herself described by an irate parent as a Nazi, a Satanist, and a Communist. The Concerned Citizens group has sought more formal ties with Citizens for Excellence in Education, Robert Simonds' group.

WHAT TO DO?

Begging the question that we have a crisis in education (Gerald Bracy and Michael Kibbey say testing experts and reporters are the ones who can't read), what can be done about the gridlock of reform caused by opposition by conservatives and evangelicals?

The Prichard Committee for Academic Excellence, outspoken supporters of Kentucky's three-year-old school reform law, decided to ask some focus groups (ninety-two people in three Kentucky towns) what they thought about the need for school reform. "Kentucky educators and policymakers have a long way to go in convincing the public, especially teachers and students, of the central premise of OBE that all children can learn. If all Kentuckians now believed all children can learn at high levels, schools would soon make a fundamental change in the way they are structured."

The report paints a complicated picture of the extent to which the public and local educators are accepting change and touches on difficult social issues that also color the fate of reform. (Keep in mind that Kentucky has a sizable minority population, mostly black.) School reform, according to the report, has become "an arena for pointing fingers over the unsatisfactory performance of schools." Most adults in the focus groups, including teachers, blamed uninterested parents for poor school performance. Students often blamed themselves and cited apathy as a cause. Most school officials in the focus groups tried to steer the conversation from blame to solutions.

The most glaring result of the study was that "most of the participants do not agree with the basic notion that all students can learn at high levels." Another hurdle for reform is many local residents' tendency to see themselves as consumers of school services rather than as part of a community that must band together to make a change (*Daily Report Card*, 1993).

Kentucky's Educational Reform Act created seventy-five Valued Outcomes (not subject specific), which by law will be performance-tested at grades four, eight, and twelve. If the school's results exceed the state expectation, it gets a financial award; if it falls below expectations, the state may take over the school. Kentucky's Reform Act is one of the more powerful efforts, nationwide, that touches on the community's role in public education, but, according to the Prichard Committee's report, its implementation so far has not interrupted the typical pattern of school-community relations.

A quite different approach was taken by the Iowa Business, Labor and Education Roundtable, a group that has pushed for better schools. The Iowa Department of Education in May abandoned its attempt to set statewide student performance goals because the effort had become too controversial (Siebert, 1993b). William Lepley, the department director who had supported such reforms as "student outcomes," "multiculturalism," and "global education," resigned. (Keep in mind that only 2 percent of Iowa's citizens are nonwhite.)

Jamie Vollmer, director of operations for the roundtable, recently finished a thirty-one–stop tour of Iowa during which he asked groups what schools should teach children. Vollmer now says Iowans are beginning to recognize the need for significant change in the state's 397 public school districts.

At the meetings, Vollmer asked the crowd to split into small groups and to make three lists: what should students know when they graduate, what should they be able to do, and what values schools should reinforce? His seminars attracted 5000 people statewide (Siebert, 1993a).

Reaching consensus wasn't easy. Abortion, crime, student discipline, and other hot-button topics dominated discussions. The point Vollmer attempts to drive home is that schools must turn out students prepared for the changing work force. Rather than demanding more from the current educational system—adding computer skills and technical literacy to the curriculum—the system must drastically be changed.

Many Iowans, who see studies regularly showing that Iowa students are at the top of the educational heap, don't see the need for drastic measures. Another argument is that schools must simply return to the basics of reading, writing, and arithmetic.

> Vollmer tires of the "back-to-basics" argument. "The traditional basics aren't enough," he said. "Computer literacy is not on the list of traditional basics. Well, it's in the top five every single time in these lists."
>
> He also disagrees that an outcome-based model has to be controversial. "If everybody gets to decide what the outcome is going to be, and the teachers know what the community expects," he said, "well, then where's the beef against the system?"
>
> Vollmer said the beauty of a system driven by the community defining what graduates should know and be able to do is that one area may decide to get to its goals much differently than another.
>
> In the end, it will be the competitive nature of Iowa towns that will bring about the changes, he said. "That competitive impulse will move the entire state forward." (Siebert, 1993a)

Vollmer said he sensed that Iowans are beginning to recognize the need for significant change. He also had some good things to say about the Religious Right: "Give them credit for being involved—they were the ones turning out on those frigid winter nights, even holding meetings the night before I arrived to get 'ready for me!' They *care* even though we may not think the same way" (Vollmer, telephone interview, December 30, 1993).

Vollmer also made available the values chosen at three of his larger meetings. Despite the common perception that values are taboo for public school curricula, they were always the longest list returned at his seminars. Table 4.1 contains the values and

Table 4.1. Values schools should reinforce.

Question: The family has the primary responsibility for teaching values. What values do you think the schools should reinforce?	
Value	Percent of Participants
Do to others what you would have them do to you	2
Honesty	50
Respect for:	
other people	44
without agreeing	2
other people's property	12
parents	3
other people's ideas	2
other people's religions	2
other people's beliefs	2
privacy	2
peers	1
Responsibility for actions	44
Self-worth and -esteem	25
Hard work (work ethic)	13
Integrity	11
Management of time	10
understanding deadlines	10
No values should be taught at all	9
Participation in democracy	9
Abstinence	
sex	8
drugs	2
alcohol	2
Respect of authority	7
Self-motivation	7
Loyalty	6

Source: Jamie Vollmer. Iowa Business, Labor, and Education Roundtable Seminars, Fall 1993.

percentages of people attending, who selected the values as ones that the schools should reinforce. Honesty, respect for other people, responsibility for our actions, and self-worth and self-esteem were most often selected. Respect for peers and abstinence from drugs and alcohol were least selected. Table 4.2 provides common dictionary definitions for the terms, which were never defined by the participants.

Starting the Communication

About the only insight that I share with Phyllis Schlafly is that our education jargon is getting in the way. The lack of understanding certainly cuts both ways, and the friction is felt by both sides. Matthew Moen calls the conflict the "Preacher versus the Teacher" (Moen, 1993). Educators assume that those with a literal understanding of the Bible cannot have a particularly high I.Q. ("How can any thinking person blithely ignore fossils?" Moen asks tongue in cheek.) Fundamentalists exhibit the same lack of understanding, assuming that there is a monolithic force indoctrinating children in "leftist" or Satanistic causes. Make no mistake about it, this genuine lack of understanding will imperil the quality of American public life for a long time because neither side will soon vacate the public square (Moen, 1993). A step in the right direction is to illuminate the existing state of affairs. Those of us charged with preparing the next generation of educators or running public schools must come to understand the shifting nature of the Fundamentalists' constituency, the infighting that is now going on among conservatives, and the changes in the Right's language and tactics since the time of the Bush 1985 presidential campaign. We must especially come to recognize and respect the uniform rise in the political sophistication of its leaders [5]. We should not expect the Fundamentalists to be "convinced" of OBE, Goals 2000, standards, or new forms of assessment, nor should we expect them to offer any acceptable alternatives. Harry and Bonano Overstreet warn in their book, *The Strange Tactics of Extremism,* "All extremists, we must realize, whether to the left or right, would rather demolish than reform."

Table 4.2. Definition of values.

1.	Value:	Worth in usefulness or importance to the possessor; utility or merit.
2.	Honesty:	The capacity or condition of being honest; integrity; trustworthiness. Truthfulness; sincerity.
3.	Respect:	To feel or show esteem for; to honor. To show consideration for; to relate or refer to; to concern.
4.	Property:	Ownership. A possession, or possessions collectively. Something tangible or intangible to which its owner has legal title.
5.	Idea:	That which exists in the mind, potentially or actually, as a product of mental activity, such as thought or knowledge; a thought; conception.
6.	Religion:	The expression of man's belief in and reverence for a superhuman power recognized as the creator and governor of the universe.
7.	Beliefs:	The mental act, condition, or habit of placing trust or confidence in a person or thing; faith. Mental acceptance or conviction in the truth or actuality of something.
8.	Privacy:	The condition of being secluded or isolated from the view of, or from contact with, others. Concealment; secrecy.
9.	Peers:	Persons who have equal standing with another, as in rank, class, age or accomplishment. A companion; fellow.
10.	Responsibility:	The state, quality or fact of being responsible. A thing or person that one is answerable for; a duty, obligation, or burden.

(continued)

Table 4.2. (continued).

11.	Self-worth:	The regarding of pride in oneself, in one's own opinion. An opinion one has in the value of his/her own being or accomplishments.
12.	Esteem:	To regard as of a high order; think of with respect; prize. Favorable regard; respect.
13.	Work ethic:	A principle one has of a desire or will for successful accomplishment of c physical or mental effort or activity directed toward the production or accomplishment of something. Accomplishment of something with favorable diligence.
14.	Integrity:	Rigid adherence to a code of behavior; probity. The state of being unimpaired; soundness. Completeness; unity.
15.	Deadline:	A time limit, as for payment of a debt or completion of an assignment.
16.	Participation in democracy:	The act of taking part of, in sharing with others, of partaking, of becoming involved in with others in a social condition of equality and respect for the individual within the community.
17.	Abstinence:	Denial of the appetites; abstention. The restraint of one's appetites or desires. The willful avoidance of pleasures thought to be harmful in some way.
18.	Respect of authority:	To feel or show esteem for; to honor a person or group invested with the right or power to command, enforce laws, exact obedience, determine, or judge. To show consideration for a person or group invested with a right or power over oneself.
19.	Self-motivation:	The act or process of motivating made by oneself or itself, one one's or it's own initiative. Self imposed desire or purpose to stimulate to action; provide with an incentive or motive.
20.	Loyalty:	The state of quality of being loyal. Feelings of devoted attachment and affection. Steadfast in allegiance to.

Source: Values from Iowa Roundtable Seminars, Fall 1993. Definitions from *American Heritage Dictionary*.

Goals 2000

The Goals 2000 approach set in motion in 1989 is working. Richard Riley is proving to be a skillful Secretary of Education who learned the politics of education well during his two terms as South Carolina's governor. The work now underway by the various scholarly groups, i.e., geography, English, history, etc., is of high quality and should have the same beneficial effects as did the 1989 mathematics standards. Where superintendents, curriculum directors, and professors of curriculum, instruction, and supervision can help the most is to develop in each state "helping relations to enable individual districts and groups of districts to effectively infuse the new curriculum content and recommendations for assessment into their existing instructional delivery systems." In addition, much more must be done to help school board members understand the necessary steps needed at the local school and district to make Goals 2000 a reality.

Assessment and Report Cards

The experiences of districts such as Littleton, Colorado, and Jackson, Wyoming, are instructive. Both districts have crackerjack staffs and enviable reputations as quality school organizations. Each of them, working at their own pace and toward their own goals, proposed real school transformation. From the backlash each experienced, it is apparent that their patrons weren't ready for that much change. It isn't simply a matter of cost, either. Gastonia, North Carolina, even with two million dollars from outside, met the same stiff resistance.

In the Hippocratic Oath, medical doctors are reminded, "First of all do no harm!" Parents (and those who self-select to speak for parents) want the same assurance. Make sure that a child's education doesn't get worse as you tinker with a school to make it better. Those who would "design down and plan up" should (1) keep standardized testing (perhaps only matrix testing for a sample) to assure that quality, as parents understand it, doesn't go down. (2) Add criteria-referenced testing as the recommendations from the National Educational Standards Improvement

Council are infused. Next, enrich the mix of assessment with performance testing following the suggestions of the particular scholarly body that created the new curriculum standards. Performance testing, as a routine part of a new curriculum, is much less fearful than a 200-page, high-stakes requirement handed to students as seniors. (3) Despite the expectation that OBE will cause academic subjects to go away, don't believe it or even talk about it. I have studied core, fusion, and integrated curriculum attempts for forty years and, except for the primary grades, teachers just can't pull it off! (4) The conventional report card is equally resilient. Parents want to know three things from their child's progress report: (a) How is my child doing in regard to his/her ability? (b) How is my child doing against the competition? (c) How will my child do in future academic endeavors? Educators know that much more information is really needed to help the child and to truly inform the parent. Unfortunately, like the Carnegie Unit and the multiple choice test, the letter grade report card simply will not die. (Perhaps we brought it on ourselves because educators have stonewalled so well as we have explained to each generation how an A− is better than a B+.)

Perhaps the best solution is to keep a conventional report card and supplement it with a more meaningful report of student *learning* process. Several adequate microcomputer programs can do this, such as *MacSchool, Performance Plus,* and *Abacus.* Eventually, the letter grade report card can be dropped. During the transition period, the district will have time to answer the usual questions: But what about grade point average? Rank in class? The honor society? Admission to Harvard?

CENSORSHIP OVER CHARGES OF NEW AGE RELIGION AND SATANISM

When I first began studying the complaints of the Fundamentalists about New Age religion taking root in the public schools, I dismissed the charges as nonsense. Now, after a year and a half of study and really trying to listen, I realize that there are two facets to the New Age movement: the occult and the humanistic. On the occult side, New Age is expressed in reincarnation, crystal power, channeling spirit guides, UFOs, extraterrestrials, and worship of self. The humanistic expression is intent on developing unlimited human potential and an ethical system centered in responsibility only to one's self.

The occult New Age Movement is faddish—and is often trivialized by calling Jerry Brown and Shirley MacLaine "space cadets." The faddish parts of the New Age Movement come and go not unlike hula hoops, but great numbers of people are energetic devotees, and the fad will last a long while because of that. The *humanistic* facet will last a long time because it has "so much to offer" to so many seeking some sort of "salvation" outside of the more established American churches. The New Age Movement is a mixture of secularism, Eastern religion, humanistic psychology, superstition, ancient and medieval witchcraft, and pagan pantheism.

In talking with clergy in our college town, I have found that most agree with Rev. Philip Lochhaas' assessment:

> It is incumbent on Christian people to recognize that in defining God out of existence and moving human beings into God's place, the New Age Movement is religious to the core and is fundamentally hostile to every Christian belief. But the task of the Christian church is not merely to lament and denounce the movement, but to minister to the vacuum in people's lives on which the movement feeds. (Lochhaas, 1988)

Pastors and heads of church-related schools would counsel their public school friends thusly: "If a public school is to be truly neutral on religion, the possible infiltration of any religious teaching is a matter of concern. Public school administrators must guard against such infiltration, whether by recognized or by obscure religions."

When public school administrators are unfamiliar with Eastern religion, for example, they may be blindsided by charges of, "You are allowing books that indoctrinate our children in a religion not of their choosing!"

Do your homework—get acquainted with religions outside of the mainstream. Perhaps you can't visit a series of churches "when your pastor is on holiday," but you can read. The Lutheran Church (Missouri Synod) has published a series of "how to respond" books, which will give you a considerable background on cults, Satanism, New Age, Secular Humanism, Islam, etc. You don't need to be a Lutheran to understand the background sections of the books—ask a Lutheran friend, who can probably borrow them from the church library.

As to censorship, contact your own association (ASCD, AAUP, AASA, or the principals' associations). You will have to dig in your heels and fight it with your school board's help. Inform the community about the procedures used for determining selection and use of educational trends. Make it clear that books and nonprint materials that meet selection criteria should not be excluded based on controversial subject matter or because of doctrinal disapproval.

MULTICULTURALISM AND GLOBALISM

Defenders of the nation's dominant culture (not all members of the Religious Right, by the way) often confuse multiculturalism for two very different social movements—what Professor Betty Jean Craige of the University of Georgia calls "globalism" and "ethnic preservationism"—because their effect on curricula are similar. Both place racial and ethnic issues in the foreground (Craige, 1994).

Ethnic preservation is the drive by minority groups to recover, preserve, and celebrate their distinct cultural identities. It's a resistance to cultural amalgamation that results from integration. Special beers at the pub on St. Patrick's Day, Cinco de Mayo Day, and Scandinavian Days are more than reasons for a sale at the mall. The dominant culture understands (or tolerates) these little quirks, but has trouble with demands for separate dormitories or student centers for various racial and ethnic groups on a campus.

Academic globalists, on the other hand, promote public awareness of human diversity. Teaching globalism means seeing the world as a community of interdependent peoples, some of whom have been dominated by others. Such lessons give priority to no single culture.

Again, to defenders of the nation's dominant culture, globalists and ethnic preservationists are both intent on empowering racial and ethnic minorities; thus, they are clumped together as "multiculturalists" and are seen as threatening. Craige has an interesting way to explain this threat (Craige, 1994). "From the perspective of the guardians of the dominant culture, the ethnic preservationists are insubordinate in being loyal to each other and the globalists are insubordinate in not being loyal to anyone!" Defenders of the dominant culture define patriotism as pride in this nation's superiority over other nations [6].

Former Education Secretary William J. Bennett argued for traditional Western Civilization humanities programs because he said the West had "set the moral, political, economic and social standards for the rest of the world." His unstated assumption was that instruction in the aesthetic and political ideas of nonwestern cultures would diminish Americans' appreciation for their own society. Mr. Bennett, Rush Limbaugh, and other critics of multicultural education consider it incompatible with patriotism.

Again, what should leaders of educational reform do? Recognize that multiculturalism is incompatible with patriotism if patriotism is defined as belief in the United States' superiority over other nations. Critiquing long-standing "truths" about our nation's past, the recognition of racial prejudice in our laws and customs, and analyses of the value systems of diverse societies, including those hostile to our own, will stimulate questioning of cultural and governmental authority.

Indeed, this will reduce the patriotism of "our country right or wrong," but it might serve, as former United States Attorney General Ramsey Clark said, to "motivate the whole country to be as good a neighbor in the community of nations as the conscience of individuals motivates them to be in communities where they live."

AIDS, PREMARITAL SEX, AND CONDOMS

It's likely you have seen Tom Hanks and Denzel Washington in the movie *Philadelphia*. It's a powerful story of a young, promising lawyer who contracts AIDS and is fired from his highly paid job at a respected law firm. Washington is the hard-knuckled ambulance chaser who helps him sue his former employers. Washington's character is also bitterly homophobic. Seeing *Philadelphia* with a college-age crowd is quite informative.

The crowd waits for the film to start, using the time to chat with friends and making the usual smart-mouth wisecracks that make the experience of attending even more entertaining.

However, once the show starts, the audience falls silent. Even before that time, the house is full. As the crowd leaves at the end of the film, everyone seems to have enjoyed the film, but no one says anything. Complete silence—some people in tears—no comments are made to the students in the long line waiting for the second show.

AIDS is the defining event for the twenty-something crowd just as Vietnam was for their parents and World War II was for their grandparents. Fear of sexually transmitted AIDS is worse than the fear we knew regarding draft numbers—our own or that of a special boyfriend. Fear of AIDS is worse than fear of going overseas to combat. Fear of AIDS has many receptive to hearing about the value of postponing sex until marriage.

This chapter started with reciting recent school news headlines. Let's close with a few regarding the issue of AIDS protection: "True Love Waits," "Chastity Campaign Has Teens Warming up to Abstinence," "White Illegitimacy Epidemic," "Virginity Is Not a Dirty Word," and "Court Rules NYC Condom Plan Violates Parent Right to Know."

A campaign urging youth to postpone sex until marriage, started by the Southern Baptist Sunday School Board as an adjunct to its sex education program, has spread rapidly to other denominations. The "True Love Waits" campaign recently hit its first goal of eliciting chastity vows from half a million teenagers. The campaign's biggest boost to date came when the 59 million-member Roman Catholic Church came on board.

The campaign uses pledge cards, which are displayed in long lines around the country. Such a display not only helps young people convince their peers that chastity before marriage is OK, but it also sends a message to political and school officials developing sex education programs.

Practicing safe sex or having no sex? Both are needed. In a recent Roper Poll of teen sex, 44 percent of thirteen to seventeen year olds disagreed that it is wrong to have sex before marriage; 28 percent said that they had engaged in sexual intercourse.

Equally frightening are the national figures on illegitimacy. The aggregate statistic for the most recent year with complete data, 1991, was 1.2 million children born to unmarried mothers, about 30 percent of all live births. Thirty percent was the black illegitimacy rate that prompted Daniel Patrick Moynihan to sound the alarm back in the 1960s, predicting the breakdown of the black family. The 1991 figures for blacks is that illegitimacy has now reached 68 percent of births to black women.

Among white women, the same figure was 22 percent in 1991. The proportion of single mothers with less than a high school education has jumped to 48 percent from 35 percent in a single decade. For white women below the poverty line, 44 percent of the births are illegitimate, compared with only 6 percent for women above the poverty line.

Charles Murray, who gathered all of these statistics for an Op. Ed. piece (Murray, 1994) predicts an emerging white underclass in our society with devastating social consequences. How much illegitimacy can a community tolerate? Murray notes that the trend lines on black crime, dropout from the labor force, homelessness, and illegitimacy all shifted sharply upward as the overall black illegitimacy rate passed 25 percent.

Illegitimacy is probably the most important social problem of our time—more important than crime, drugs, poverty, illiteracy, welfare, and homelessness—because it drives everything else. Murray makes a powerful argument for making marriage paramount again. His proposal is to end all economic support for single mothers in order to restigmatize bearing children out of wedlock.

> In the calculus of illegitimacy, the constants are that boys like to sleep with girls and that girls think babies are endearing. Human societies have historically channeled these elemental forces of human behavior via thick walls of rewards and penalties that constrained the overwhelming majority of births to take place in marriage. The past 30 years have seen those walls cave in. It is time to rebuild them.
>
> The ethical underpinning for the policies I am about to describe is this: bringing a child into the world is the most important thing that most human beings ever do. Bringing a child into the world

when one is not emotionally or financially prepared to be a parent is wrong. The child deserves society's support. The parent does not. (Murray, 1994)

Murray's idea of rebuilding the thick walls of rewards and punishment may at first blush seem impossible to do. Yet that is exactly what the battle between "the teacher and the preacher is all about." For conflict to lead to consensus, we must agree on common ideals.

Americans do have differing views on the issues. Clearly, religious consensus in the United States is not likely. A consensus that we can share *as citizens* is possible and necessary. We must agree on certain principles that unite us as a nation.

Much more needs to be said about the underlying philosophical assumptions that are being made as we transform our schools to be world-class. What constitutes "fairness" as we teach history, literature, culture? Public school leaders are probably trying too hard to be neutral. Exclusion of religious perspectives is anything but neutral or fair. Students need to know that religious practices and philosophical beliefs are central to the lives of many people.

If we are to ever find that middle, *common* ground, educators must accept what is valid about criticisms of methodology and curriculum. At the same time, those on the "preacher" side of the battle must come to accept that most teachers and administrators do not intend to promote a secular or New Age world view. In the end, we will not exclude all religious perspectives, nor will we establish one religion–Christianity–over all others. "Both have been tried in various places and times in our history and both were found to violate the spirit and the letter of the First Amendment" (Haynes, 1993).

ENDNOTES

1. The five secretaries were speaking at the third annual Secretaries' Roundtable sponsored by the College Board, the Southern Center for International Studies, and the Georgia Institute of Technology, where the Forum was held. The program aired on Public Broadcasting Service stations on

January 16, 1994. (1) Ms. Hufstedler was the first Secretary of Education (Carter administration) followed by (2) Bell (Reagan) (3) Bennett (Reagan), (4) Cavazos (Reagan), and (5) Alexander (Bush).
2. Indeed, most of the other nations whose world-class educational systems we covet use such examinations.
3. FIRST grants are from the Fund for the Improvement and Reform of Schools and Teaching, administered by the United States Department of Education.
4. Littleton, Colorado, has nineteen graduation requirements measured by thirty-six "performance demonstrations." When Littleton High students registered last fall, they received a 200-page book describing the required demonstrations.
5. The Religious Right claims to have its own ACLU, the Rutherford Institute founded in 1982 in Virginia, which now has thirty chapters.
6. This attribute is best exemplified by a Lake County school board in Tavares, Florida, that has decreed that its teachers must tell its students that the American Culture is superior to all others now—and throughout history!

REFERENCES

American Association of School Administrators. 1992. *The Study of the American School Superintendency.* Arlington, VA: The Association.

1993. "Barney a Demon?" *Chicago Tribune* (November 26):16.

Bennett, W. J. 1992. *The Devaluing of America: The Fight for Our Culture and Our Children.* New York: Summit Books.

Bingham, J. 1993. "The 3 R's: Parents Wage War," *The Sunday Denver Post* (December 12):1, 14A.

1993. "Bluegrass State: Education Reform Faces Obstacles," *Daily Report Card* (October 28):3(105):3.

Commission on Standards for School Mathematics. 1989. *Curriculum and Evaluation Standards for School Mathematics.* Reston, VA: National Council of Teachers of Mathematics.

Craige, B. J. 1994. "Multiculturalism and the Vietnam Syndrome," *The Chronicle of Higher Education,* 20(19):B3.

Dewell, T. 1993. "Goals Split Local Community," *Jackson Hole News* (December 8):1.

Haynes, C. C. 1993. "Beyond the Culture Wars," *Educational Leadership,* 51(2):30–34.

Lochhaas, P. H. 1988. *How to Respond to the New Age Movement.* St. Louis: Concordia Publishing House.

Manatt, R. P. 1993. "The Attack by the U.S. Religious Right on 'Government Schools,' " *International Journal of Educational Reform* (October):443–455.

Moen, M. C. 1993. "The Preacher versus the Teacher," *NEA Higher Education Journal*, 9(1):125–143.

Murray, C. 1994. "White Illegitimacy Epidemic–American Cannot Survive It," *Des Moines Sunday Register* (January 2):1, 2c.

National Committee on Science Education Standards and Assessment. 1993. *National Science Education Standards: An Enhanced Sampler.* Washington, D.C.: National Research Council.

1994. "Outcomes-Based Education: Connecticut's Tug of War," *Daily Report Card* (January 10):3:139:2.

Overstreet, H. and B. Overstreet. 1964. *The Strange Tactics of Extremism.* New York: W. W. Norton and Company.

Pisch, M. 1994. "Standards Issue Puts Ex-Education Secretaries at Odds," *Education Week* (January 12):20.

Schlafly, P. 1993. "What's Wrong with Outcomes-Based Education," *American Family Action Journal* (November/December):20–23. The Family Action Coalition, P.O. Box 1043, Belton, MO 64012.

Siebert, M. 1993a. "Overhaul Inevitable? Stoking Debate on School Reform," *The Des Moines Register* (December 27):7, 8B.

Siebert, M. 1993b. "Statewide Education Goals Dropped," *The Des Moines Register* (May 7):1.

Sommerfield, M. 1993a. "Christian Activists Seek to Torpedo NASDC Project," *Education Week* (March 10):1–18.

Sommerfield, M. 1993b. "Crossroads Academy Funds Arts Programs in Public Schools," *Education Week* (October 20):A4.

Varnum, C. J. and R. L. King. 1993. "A Tidal Wave of Change–OBE in the U.S.A.," *Outcomes,* 12(1):16–19.

Viandro, D. 1993a. "Projects to Explore Integrating Standards for the Early Grades," *Education Week* (April 7):16.

Viandro, D. 1993b. "Study Finds U.S. Schools Lag in Learning Attitudes," *Education Week* (April 7):16.

1993. "What's In and Out in 1993," *Education Week* (January 13):43.

Young, M. W. 1993a. "Countdown. The Goals 2000: Educate America Act," *National Forum,* 73(4):3–4.

Young, M. W. 1993b. "National Priorities for Education: A Conversation with U.S. Secretary of Education, Richard W. Riley," *National Forum,* 73(4):5–7.

CHAPTER 5

Survival and Victory in the School Culture Wars

WHERE will it all end? Public education is responsible for the transmission of the ideals, knowledge, and values of our American way of life. These same schools are expected to avoid undermining parents' moral and religious teaching. Former Deputy Secretary of Education, Diane Ravich, calls the period this book has described as "the great school wars." At the present time, the initiative seems to be with the Fundamentalists.

Schools are self-censoring materials, teaching methods, and activities so as not to raise the ire of the Religious Right. Public schools are considered by many "morally dangerous places for children."

Schools have bent over backwards for so long in their efforts not to offend anyone about anything that there is nothing left in the curriculum even vaguely resembling religious or ethical content. Kern Ryan, a Boston University professor of education, concludes that the result is a historical, boring, misleading, and morally dangerous experience for children (Merrow, 1994, p. 56). Schools didn't become a battleground overnight. Merrow blames it on years of a high-level policy of *cowardice*. Values, he points out, are being taught now: the values of "don't rock the boat."

Merrow, in his essay "Don't Offend: Our High Level Policy of Cowardice," puts it bluntly that the current educational posture–retreat from controversy–offends nearly everyone. Where are the leaders who will restore religion to its rightful place in the teaching of our history–and at the same time stand up to the extremists who would impose their values on all our children?

FUNDAMENTALISTS' STRATEGY

In any war, strategy is important. What is the strategy of the Fundamentalists?

1. *Taking over our school boards*—Fundamentalists are running for school boards all over the country with considerable success. This pattern started in the 1980s and became the testing ground for later efforts to take over the state-level GOP. Because of stealth tactics, the number of board members who are Fundamentalists is not easy to verify. It is known that they have captured board majorities in California, Texas, Florida, Colorado, and Louisiana. Most states have scores of boards with at least one member.

   The stealth approach works likes this. First of all, a little known candidate runs for the board campaigning on a platform that stresses traditional values and a back-to-the-basics approach. The candidate promises to make schools "safe, orderly places" and to cut the budget. The hidden part of the agenda is to foster Fundamentalists' causes. Then, the newly seated board member, to everyone's surprise, begins attacking the whole alphabet of affective education through whole-language learning.

   Often, a potluck dinner is held in a Fundamentalist church where secret supporters have been working for months to increase the votes among congregants. The traditional disinterest in local elections works to the advantage of this strategy because one busload of church members sent to the polling places can often swing the election.

2. *Forming pressure groups*—Anyone who has spent a lifetime attending school board meetings can attest to the low attendance and disinterest generally shown by the public. Consequently, it doesn't take much of a crowd to surprise and impress the school board. Fundamentalist groups form a local pressure group to attend board meetings and make demands on the members.

   Again, the pressure group joins a sparsely attended meeting and, by its numbers, hopes to convince boards that they represent a majority sentiment. Most often, the group challenges sex education, antidrug, or self-esteem programs. A favorite request (which often leaves board members scratching their heads) is that all teacher-made tests given to children be sent home for parents to see. The suggestion is made saying, "That's what they do in Japan and the mothers can really help the students that way." Apparently, some national religious groups believe that, by finding tests or test questions that deal with values and beliefs used in several states, they can build the case for a Supreme Court challenge. Not surprisingly, teachers who have worked long and hard on an assessment resent the loss of test security that this request entails.

Phyllis Schlafly's Eagle Forum also assists Fundamentalists with local pressure tactics. The Forum provides a list of school activities deemed "offensive." The Forum suggests that the parent groups should demand that their children be allowed to opt out. Many of the so-called "offensive" items are so vague that they can cover most of what public schools do. Again, they have found a perfect "catch 22" to harass school officials.

3. *Supporting vouchers* – Convincing a majority of Americans to vote for vouchers requires more than a pro-voucher campaign. Perhaps all of the attacks on public education in the past few years have a very simple goal: to build public support for private school vouchers. Puzzling as it may seem, the Fundamentalists no longer fear government control will come with government money. Somehow, the Religious Right has put aside concerns for government control and has jumped on the vouchers band wagon.

So far, the voucher band wagon hasn't gone anywhere. Americans in both polls and in test elections have shown a great wariness regarding vouchers. It's likely that Fundamentalists believe that tearing down the public school, and thereby convincing the American parent and taxpayer that public schools "espouse secular humanism" and "New Age religion" and are not safe for children, will help move the voucher band wagon along.

Arnold Fege of the National PTA believes that these issues (sex education; drug abuse; charges of lazy, inept public school teachers) are unifying the far right and other groups that oppose public education. "They unify on vouchers and they unify around a lot of bogus information about OBE and sex education. This is a well-orchestrated campaign around a well developed range of issues that are unifying a segment of our population" (Boston, 1994, p. 20).

4. *Control of the Republican party* — It remains to be seen whether the Fundamentalists and their anti-school colleagues can succeed in general elections. There is no question that their strategies include taking over party machinery. The years of disillusionment with Reagan and Bush are past. While they have no obvious first choice as a presidential candidate, Fundamentalists have a wealth of hopefuls: Robert Dole, senator from Kansas and Senate minority leader; Lamar Alexander, former governor of Tennessee; Phil Gramm, senator from Texas; Jack Kemp, former housing secretary; and Dick Cheney, former defense secretary, are the early front runners. Certainly, Pat Buchanan and Pat Robertson will also try again.

One thing they are all united on is a dislike of a liberal President and a liberal Congress. Phil Gramm spoke at the June 1994, Republican State Convention in Iowa where the 1996 presidential campaign has begun. "I find a lot of Republicans who are wishing that we could skip 95 and go right to 96. They want 96 to come so that Clinton can go" (Krasky, 1994, p. A19).

Pat Buchanan spoke directly to the Fundamentalists' theme for 1996, "America's social crisis is rooted in our moral crisis, which is rooted in a spiritual crisis. The party needs a vision that is rooted in Judeo-Christian values and traditional conservative Republican principles."

When Senator Arlen Specter of Pennsylvania cautioned that the GOP has no business excluding anyone over issues such as abortion and gay rights, he was booed (Krasky, 1994).

Previously, Robert Simonds, president of the Citizens for Excellence in Education, explained how serious he believes the threat of liberalism to be in his annual *President's Report*.

"This year, 1993, is the most critical year of the next four years of a liberal Congress and liberal President. They can pass any liberal bill they choose to pass. You and your children must then live under that yoke of bondage which could destroy not only what you believe in, but could totally alienate your own children through your schools' liberal, socialistic indoctrination."

To Reverend Simonds and his allies the passage of Goals 2000: Educate America must be the ultimate proof of a world gone sour. Despite the "voluntary" nature of the standards and assessment recommendations in the Act, the huge sums of money involved will induce most public school districts to apply. Once again, we will see the attacks at the state level similar to those in Kentucky over the Kentucky Education Reform Act and in Iowa regarding Outcome-Based Education. States must have a plan before individual districts may apply. Thus, the state will be the first target. As this is written, Iowa school officials are struggling with meeting the Goals 2000 application requirements without reawakening the Fundamentalists. No doubt, Governor Terry Branstad prefers not to appoint a planning board until the November election. He has decided to postpone any application until December 1994.

The distribution of the funds from Goals 2000 will also stir the passions of the Fundamentalists. After 1994, when 40% of the funds stay at the state level for start-up costs, the distribution will be 10% for the state, 5% for the local education agency, and 85% to the building. Considering that the intent of Goals 2000 is a robust curriculum renewal and assessment to be sure students are learning the new content in skills, the tendency of district offices to structure "Goals" activities uniformly across buildings should give the Fundamentalists plenty to complain about. The charge will be loss of local control and the imposition of a national curriculum. Fundamentalists also detest site-based management.

A little discussed or even understood condition of the receipt of funds, delivery standards, now called opportunity to learn (OTL), will be even more controversial. Opportunity to learn data are to be assembled to prove that a district or a state is being even-handed about the use of Goals 2000 money. The inclusion of two new goals, training for teachers and parental involvement, should provide even more targets for the Religious Right.

BELIEFS OF FUNDAMENTALISTS

A large population of Americans are Christian. Keep in mind that only a small percentage of the total Christian group agrees with the beliefs of the Religious Right and actually work to further their agenda. The religious identity of American Christians and their percentages are presented in Figure 5.1.

The Horace Mann League, a patriotic and educational group comprised of school administrators and professors of education, has completed a list of general beliefs of Fundamentalists. Those that relate to public education are as follows (Hammond et al., 1993, p. 3):

- We Christians can more effectively apply biblical principles to government because we read the Bible and trust its teaching.
- We believe books in classrooms and libraries that include "anti-biblical" language or any reference to the occult should be banned.

Identity	Beliefs
Moderates to Liberals (42%)	"are main-line Protestants for whom progressive social action is the very essence of Christian witness."
Evangelicals (24%)	"believe in the authority of the Bible, but some may view it as symbolic, not historical."
Fundamentalists (21%)	"strongly oppose liberalism in society; believe the Bible is the perfect word of God and historically true; expect that after several catastrophic events, Jesus will return to set up a literal kingdom."
Charismatic or Pentecostal (12%)	"find authority but not always literal truth in the Bible, believe in modern day miracles, and emphasize spiritual gifts such as speaking in tongues."

FIGURE 5.1 Religious identity and percentage of Christians (source: U.S.A. Today, March 25, 1993, p. 1D).

Beliefs of Fundamentalists 129

- We believe public schools teach no absolutes, no God, no wrong or right.
- Societal ills that we have today are reflected in our public school classrooms.
- The Bible empowers Godly Christians with the right to supervise the teaching of our children.
- For America to be saved, the people have to return to patriotic and conservative domestic policies (i.e., ban abortions, constitutionally reinstitute school prayer, maintain military strength, and outlaw pornography).
- "Secular humanism" and other "anti-God" philosophies must be driven from public schools and replaced with God-centered morality.
- It is the Lord's plan to bring public education back under the control of the Christian community.
- If public schools cannot be brought back to God, then we believe they must be replaced by private schools or home schooling.
- We must win elections to gain majority seats on every city council and school board.
- There is only one interpretation of the Bible. It is directly inspired by God and literally infallible.
- We believe in localism, conventional moral standards, traditionalist family values, and vocal "Americanism."

The Fundamentalist beliefs somehow get translated into "desirable" school changes, "undesirable" school reforms, and educational practices to be maintained.

1. "Desirable" school changes: school prayer, creationism, school choice, home schooling, vouchers, equal access for religious clubs, student-initiated prayer, reduction of the powers of national and state education departments, and abstinence-based sex education programs
2. "Undesirable" school reforms: affective education, self-esteem, school-based health clinics, global education, Outcome-Based Education, multiculturalism, mastery learning, site-based management, health services on campus, lengthening of the school day and year, ungraded classrooms, assessment testing, vocational education, sex education,

whole-language learning, values clarification, critical thinking skills, cooperative learning, peer coaching, teacher-as-coach, decision-making skills, AIDS or HIV education, and nontraditional report cards

3. Educational practices to be maintained: phonics, reading, mathematics, patriotism, character education, student-initiated prayer, the scholastic aptitude test, report cards, rank in class, Carnegie Unit credits, honor societies, and valedictorian and salutatorian recognition

Once more, an analysis of "what's okay" leads to the conclusion that the 1950 school is acceptable, especially if it has a strong Christian bias in all activities and content. No wonder home schooling looks so good to so many Fundamentalists.

HOME SCHOOLING

Ten years ago, choosing to educate your child at home was an indication of crankiness, a counterculture sort of thing. Now it's fashionable!

The Department of Education estimates that the number of school-age children being taught at home has risen from 1500 at the start of the 1980s to 350,000 in 1992. The Home School Legal Defense Association put the figure higher—500,000 or more. The difference is explained by the Legal Defense Association by saying home schooling parents don't like talking to the census takers.

What do we know about home schoolers? They have slightly higher incomes and much more stable families than the average American. Aside from that, they vary widely. In the Northwest, the movement started in the 1970s. These parents tend to be New Age types influenced by the antischooling ideas of A. S. Neil and Ivan Illich.

Elsewhere, particularly in the South, they are usually Fundamentalist Christians angry over the prayer ban "that keeps God out of the classroom." Home schooling has made its slightest impact in the Midwest, where, according to the *Economist,* "opting out of the local school is tantamount to opting out of local society" (*Economist,* 1994, p. B9).

New England has made it particularly difficult to do home schooling. Massachusetts, which pioneered compulsory education, imposes particularly heavy regulations, making it almost impossible.

The main reason given for most families to home school is what most see as the inadequacy of the public school, i.e., falling test scores, growing violence, lousy teachers, and most to the point, a pervasive egalitarianism, which stifles bright students.

Home schooling on a continuous basis also suggests some shortcomings of private education. Independent schools are often too expensive, while Catholic parochial schools are often so hard up they often don't have the resources of their public sector neighbors.

On the surface, home schooling does not seem to exact any academic price. Brian Ray, president of the National Education Research Institute, points out that, on standardized tests, home schoolers do as well or better than their conventionally educated peers.

How can home-schooling parents do the job? First, they make maximum use of microcomputers. Programs are available for teaching everything from algebra to zoology. Second, they have become socially acceptable; they have their own specialized magazines, a radio call-in show, and have increasingly better reports in the national media.

Should the movement worry public school advocates? "In a society where two income families are becoming the norm and where parents pay for public schools whether they use them or not, home schooling involves considerable sacrifices of both time and money" (*Economist,* 1994, p. B9). The fact that more and more parents are turning to home schools implies something inadequate about the state of public education.

LESSONS FROM LITTLETON, COLORADO; ADRIAN, MICHIGAN; AND KENTUCKY

Over time, school districts and states are learning from experience that some approaches are successful in dealing with the debate over values. Adrian, Michigan, for example, has been termed by the American Association of School Administrators as victorious in "Great School Wars." Adrian has long been recognized as a progressive, effective district in Michigan. The district had proposed a restructuring that included a new curriculum written by nationally recognized consultants and members of the district's thinking skills workshop. As usual, they were blocked by parents who saw the proposed changes as conflicting with their moral and religious teachings and what they believed to be the compact between parents and public education. Fundamentalists insist that they give up to schools only the teaching of the basics. Parents will do all else. In this instance, despite the conflict, a new trust was established through open dialogue (AASA, 1994).

The Littleton, Colorado, public schools were not as fortunate. In Chapter 4, Littleton's elaborate and thorough planning for Outcome-Based Education was described. Littleton is a largely Republican Denver suburb. The school district serves 16,000 people, 91% of them white. Like Adrian, Littleton has a reputation for fine schools. Littleton has also had a history of stable school administration and good faculty/staff board relationships. Cile Chavez had been superintendent for ten years. Before that, Robert Tschirki had been superintendent for a long time. They had hired a promising Ph.D., Tim Westerburg, to be principal of the 1175-student Heritage High School [1].

The Littleton restructuring was named Direction 2000 and the slogan "rethinking the American high school" was used. Heritage High School became a mecca for public school educators seeking information on OBE and Direction 2000. Apparently, parents and community members in the Heritage High School's attendance area were convinced that the Direction 2000's program of performance-based graduation requirements was desirable. Over eight years and thousands of hours were spent developing the learner outcomes.

In November of 1993, a trio of candidates for the school board, running on a back-to-basics slate, took control of the five-person school board. By February of 1994, Ms. Chavez was forced to resign her superintendency.

The issues in Littleton included

1. How and what teachers should teach
2. What should be expected of students
3. What role parents should play
4. How school board members should govern
5. What schools should look like at the end of the twentieth century

Two of the new board members (Bill Cisney and Carol Brzecek) had sued the District's Direction 2000 decision-making committee for holding meetings that they charged were breaking the state's Sunshine Law. As they pressed their case, they drew wide public support. Next, they asked John Fanchi to run with them. The three candidates raised tough questions. Were the new graduation requirements too tough? Were parents' complaints not listened to? Was the school venturing into uncharted territory with performance assessments?

The three challengers were supported by a group calling themselves the basic education support team (BEST). BEST wanted to see an emphasis on traditional academic areas so that "they know their children have learned the fundamentals for moving to the next grade."

After the election, to outsiders it appeared that the Fundamentalists had won another victory. A new school board had returned the district to traditional graduation requirements (Carnegie Units and grade point averages). They had nullified the requirements that Direction 2000 had set for the graduating class of 1995. Those seniors were to complete a series of demonstrations of their knowledge and skills to earn a diploma. The demonstrations were organized around stated graduation requirements (both academic subjects and goals such as critical thinking, community involvement, ethics, and human relations).

The total package contained thirty-six demonstrations with dozens of tasks. Students had to be "proficient" on seventeen of the requirements and "excellent" on two to graduate. "Proficient" was equivalent to the traditional student mark of B. Students had more than one chance to demonstrate proficiency.

While many assumed that the board was dominated by the

Fundamentalists (and their platform would suggest that), Cisney, now president of the board, denies it. He notes that he is a registered Democrat and that not all of the new board members even attend church regularly.

Nonetheless, the Religious Right was quite willing to celebrate their victory in Littleton. Phyllis Schlafly's Eagle Forum newsletter rejoiced in the slate's victory with a headline that read "OBE Trounced in Model District, Parents Vote for Three R's in a Two-to-One Mandate" [2].

Westerberg and his teachers found themselves in an increasingly common bind. They were scorned for offering programs to develop a sense of ethics in students, to insure that they could work together, and to make sure that each should do thirty hours of community service. Westerberg points out that the ability to work in groups was an outcome that business leaders had been requesting.

The new board members rejected calls for teachers to be coaches, to help students learn on their own, and to foster students' ability to work in groups. Their campaign materials made it clear "... that education is not best realized when students chart their own course, but through the active leadership of well-educated competent adults in the classroom."

Westerberg points out that teachers, or entire academic departments, can still use the demonstrations or class assignments. He hopes that, by Fall 1994, the faculty will have decided to use Direction 2000 as a set of "school wide standards" and will have worked out in detail which demonstrations will be used in which classes.

The Littleton case makes it clear that parents (or at least a huge majority of the voters) rejected many of the central tenets of the school reform movement, e.g., higher standards, new ways of assessment, depth of knowledge rather than breadth, and greater intentions of developing students' thinking and social skills. Board member Brzecek, a part-time accountant, made a telling comment, "I believe that kids need to sit through some of these classes. This program (Direction 2000) eliminated content. They spent an enormous amount of time on assessing and counseling students."

The new board is apparently finished with the high schools.

Now it's focused on the elementary schools and middle schools. Returning to the basics sounded appealing during the election; they even praised E. D. Hirsch, Jr.'s cultural literacy program. Once they tackled the subject, however, everyone seemed to have a different definition of what back-to-the-basics meant. They found that attempts to define the basics were so difficult they decided to search for "effective means of instruction."

> The board has directed Jim Weatherill, one of Chavez's deputies who is now superintendent, to come up with a proposal for reviewing how math, reading, and writing are taught and to review educational research to determine which methods and practices work. To many Littleton teachers, these actions are further indication that the school board doesn't trust or respect teachers. (Bradley, 1994, p. 24)

Elitism pervades much of the Littleton debate. Much of the attack on Direction 2000 has come from people who are successful professionals. Science teacher Kathy Dinmore says, "Any system would work for their kids. We just can't ignore the other half of the population. It seems very selfish to me—I succeeded, so I want my kids to have the same system."

To many critics, the Littleton Directions 2000 would have "watered down" student grades, making them less competitive. Doug Kenyon, head of BEST and a Cornell University engineering graduate (now a technical consultant for Marathon Oil), said, "We're very eager for our children to succeed. We see so much more stress in the work place. The opportunities are going to be much harder for our children. I see a real dog-eat-dog world out there."

KENTUCKY EDUCATIONAL REFORM ACT (KERA)

The statewide efforts to restructure schools in Kentucky provide some interesting learning points for school reform. Now that KERA has had enough time to develop seventy-five valued outcomes, has begun building a statewide computer network, and has begun assessing schools and school districts by results—not simply inputs—the usual opposition groups and arguments have risen.

Some opposition focuses on the magnitude and content of the reform act. No one doubts that KERA is a serious and courageous attempt to raise the quality of Kentucky's public schools.

Other pressure groups, with names such as "Families United for Moral Education," "Citizens United to Reform Education," and "Parents Concerned for Education," have produced the customary litany of doubt: (1) KERA is a social experiment based on unproven theories. (2) It is a form of socialism because it encourages students to work in groups. (3) The statewide computer network will result in privacy invasion regarding students' beliefs. (4) KERA opens schools to the teaching of witchcraft and homosexuality.

Defenders of KERA, such as Robert Sexton, executive director of the Prichard Committee, a group in Lexington that monitors the progress of the reform, note that this debate is quite different from the arguments over better education from the past. "This is a political debate" (Associated Press, 1994, p. B3).

KERA supporters say that critics' primary interest is not the reform act at all, but the values and moral issues that are part of schooling. Ron Hann, executive director of the Kentucky Association of School Superintendents, calls vouchers the opponents' "hidden agenda" (Associated Press, 1994).

MISINFORMATION AND THE BIGGEST HOAX

Those struggling to improve American public education have learned that the new arena is politics and "politics ain't bean bag." Benjamin Disraeli warned, "It is much easier to be critical than correct." The use of half-truths, bogus data, and outright lies on the part of the opposition to school reform is shocking to educators who have been accustomed to well-reasoned arguments backed up by sound facts and figures.

OBE is not group learning. Cooperative education does not mean socialism. Mastery learning does not mean "grade averaging." Fighting back against the unfair attacks by the Religious Right is not bigotry.

Perhaps the biggest lie of the past eighteen months uncovered in this examination of the attack by Fundamentalists is the

Misinformation and the Biggest Hoax 137

"Public Schools Problems List." Bill Bennett, George Will, and Rush Limbaugh love to cite the Public Schools Problems List.

For many veterans of the school culture wars, the striking contrast between the simple problems faced by teachers in the 1940s and the difficult problems of the 1980s was considered shocking proof of the decline of America's well-being. No doubt you have seen them on a bulletin board or listened to them gleefully read by a right-wing talk show host.

In the 1940s the problems were

1. Talking
2. Chewing gum
3. Making noise
4. Running in the halls
5. Getting out of turn in line
6. Wearing improper clothing
7. Not putting paper in wastebaskets

The top problems in the 1980s had become

1. Drug abuse
2. Alcohol abuse
3. Pregnancy
4. Suicide
5. Rape
6. Robbery
7. Assault

Barry O'Neill, an associate professor in the School of Organization and Management at Yale University, saw the list and smelled a rat. "The old-time problems seemed too trivial and the contrast between then and now too tidy" (O'Neill, 1994). He had seen other surveys of teachers regarding school problems from reputable research groups, and the contemporary problems were not nearly as serious as the schools problems list would indicate. In 1984 the Gallup Poll asked teachers to name the biggest school problems, and the top two were parent apathy and lack of financial support, but drugs were near the bottom. The National

Center for Educational Statistics asked specifically about discipline and safety issues, and the educators' major complaints were tardiness, absenteeism, and fighting. Again, drugs fell near the bottom, well below tobacco!

Puzzled by the inconsistencies, Professor O'Neill tried to locate the source of the list of problems. Everyone made use of the problems list. Not all of them were conservatives. They appeared in liberal columns, including those of Anna Quindlen, Herb Caen, and Carl Rowan. William Bennett used them in television talks, editorials, and speeches to promote his new book on America's moral decay. Dr. Joycelyn Elders, the Surgeon General, said they showed the need for social service and health programs.

O'Neill found the originator after several months. As he had suspected, the list was not scientifically valid, but neither was it intended to be a hoax. The originator had offered it merely as his opinion, with no intent to hoodwink the experts. It was later users who added all of the background detail. William Bennett, for example, claimed it was an "ongoing survey" asking teachers "the same questions" over the years. Some felt free to modify the list. Rush Limbaugh cited Bill Bennett as his authority but added a few school problems of his own!

The originator was T. Cullen Davis of Fort Worth, a born-again Christian who devised the list as a Fundamentalist attack on public schools. Sometime around 1982, Davis constructed the lists and passed them around to other Fundamentalists.

O'Neill asked him how he had arrived at his lists. "They weren't done from a scientific survey," he said. "How did I know how the offenses in school were in 1940? I was there. How do I know what they are now? I read the newspapers."

The users of Davis' list read like a Who's Who of the Fundamentalists' gurus. In addition to Bennett, Limbaugh, and George Will, the Reverend Tim LaHaye put the list in a book promoting family values. Phyllis Schlafly used the idea in an essay about her own school days. Mel and Norma Gabler, who bring you the sanitized textbook approval list from Texas, ran the list in their newsletter.

After collecting close to 200 versions of the list, O'Neill tackled the harder question, "Why have Americans found the list so attractive?" "The list is not facts but a fundamental expression of attitudes and emotions. . . . Americans today regard their country as the richest, freest, and fairest, with the best social system, but cannot square that with the social problems with America's youth."

O'Neill closes with sound advice for critics and supporters of the school reform movement:

> They [the lists] overlooked the success of American public education, its great experiences since 1940, and its high quality despite taxpayer resistance. The lists' broad sweep ignores that some public schools are devastated by violence and substance abuse and others are hardly touched at all. They should not guide our choices on educational policy. (O'Neill, 1994, p. 20)

A PLAN FOR VICTORY IN THE SCHOOLS' CULTURE WARS

The Fundamentalists' attacks are wrongheaded and have elements of racism, bigotry, and elitism. With their usual reverse image of the truth, the new defense against counterattack used by the Fundamentalists is illustrated by the letter all forty-three Republican senators recently signed and sent to President Clinton asking him to repudiate Democratic attacks on Republican religious conservatives as bigotry.

Donald Kaul, a *Des Moines Register* columnist, had an interesting view of the bigotry defense.

> I do find the Religious Right's measured response to Clinton's attacks and others richly amusing in its hypocrisy, however. "Oh my goodness they're calling us names. It's religious bigotry is what it is." This from a group that calls you a Satanist the first time you stand up to it.
>
> I think that Clinton should see if the IRS has grounds to pull the tax exemption from political groups masquerading as religious organizations. (Kaul, 1994, p. 11-A)

Educators and supporters attempting to make schools better should use Table 5.1 as a guide.

The announcement of Goals 2000: Educate America state applications in August 1994 is bound to trigger a great deal of activity, both from districts applying and Fundamentalists posturing to discredit the whole Act. The umbrella charge will be that

Table 5.1. A management action plan for successful school reform (Goals 2000: Educate America and beyond).

Time Sequence	Persons Involved	Strategy and/or Activity
First two months	Board and entire staff	Know the restructuring being proposed. What will be accomplished? How will it serve students and parents?
Third month	Board and entire staff and selected community members	Use a stakeholders' committee to study the advantages and obligations of accepting Goals 2000 funds.
First six months of Goals 2000 activity	Superintendent and cabinet	Inform the community about the proposed changes. Use no acronyms or jargon.
Goals 2000: Year I	Board and superintendent	Be focused on what your community wants for its schools. "Make It Here," "Invent It Here."
Year I	Board and superintendent	Establish a forum for debate and discussion. Why do we need more than traditional college prep?
Year I	All stakeholders	Do your homework. Subscribe to the magazines and newsletters that promote a Fundamentalist viewpoint.
Year I	Board and superintendent	Have data to support changes made. Use national standards reports.
Goals 2000: Year II		Once the reforms are launched (new content, changes in progress assessment, and reporting).
Year II	Board	A. Allow choice within the system (excuse from some experiences, transfers, open enrollment, etc.).
Year II	All stakeholders	B. Open your schools to show how changes are helping students.
Years II, III	Board and administration	B. Stand firm. You are not teaching witchcraft, you are not dumbing down the standards, but don't counterattack your critics.
All years	Board and administration	Use no labels or name calling. Don't talk down to your critics.
All years	Board and administration	Build coalitions with community church leaders, other public school districts, and universities.
All years	Board and administration	Build an ever-improving climate and create a culture of tolerance that accommodates and expects diverse points of view.
All years	Superintendent and administration	Inform students, use their input. Keep them as members of the stakeholders' group.

Table 5.1. (continued).

Time Sequence	Persons Involved	Strategy and/or Activity
All years	Board and all stakeholders	Create a program evaluation procedure that will consider criticism as another data source. Act promptly once the information is known.
All years	Board and superintendent	Make the press very welcome. Help them tie your reforms to state Goals 2000 efforts.
All years	Superintendent	Encourage visibility in the community. Sell reform like you would a bond referendum.
All years	Superintendent	Gather broad-based information from your coalition allies. Make such information a part of the board decision-making process.
All years	All stakeholders	When and if attacked by Fundamentalists: A. Discuss the First Amendment, not your or their religious beliefs. B. Provide media training for administrators, teachers, and stakeholders.
Goals 2000: Years II and III	Board and superintendent	C. Ask church leaders, business leaders, and mainstream parents to attend board meetings and forums.
All years	All stakeholders	Always use consistent, friendly language with parents.
Goals 2000: Year I	Board and superintendent	Establish policy for dealing with controversy within your school.

Goals 2000 is just OBE from the federal level. Expect the use of the term OBE to disappear. The powerful ideas implied will not disappear. Dr. Glenn Holzman, headmaster of the Northwest Academy in Houston and a skillful Christian, said recently, "I don't know what all this fuss is about. I could teach the Bible well using OBE! Finally, remember how public education works in America. Because of the residual powers inherent in our Constitution, education is a state function, a local operation, and a grave national concern! Let's pray it remains that way."

ENDNOTES

1. Both Robert Tschirki and Tim Westerburg hold doctorates from the educational administration program that the author chairs at Iowa State University. Both of them have kept the ISU faculty well informed of their Littleton experiences.
2. Perhaps the overwhelming defeat of the OBE-supporting incumbents was made possible by the new ease of voting by mail in Colorado elections. A new, mail-in ballot system encouraged 45% of Littleton's 59,000 registered voters to participate. A remarkable percentage for a nonfinancial school election.
3. Districts and state education offices will find strong support from the American Association of School Administrators, the Association for Supervision and Curriculum Development, the Educational Commission of the States, the American Library Association, and the National Association of School Boards.

REFERENCES

AASA. 1994. *Shaking the Foundations: The Conservative Christian Challenge to School Restructuring.* Audiocassette Series. Arlington, VA: American Association of School Administrators.

Associated Press. 1994. "Opposition to KERA Has Led to Forming a Slintered Front," *Lexington Herald Leader* (May):B-3.

Boston, R. 1994. "Public Schools under Seige," *Church and State,* 47(4):4–9, 20.

Bradley. 1994. "Requeim for a Reform," *Educational Week* (April):21–25.

Economist. 1994. "Classless Society: At-Home Schools Growing Trend," *The Arizona Republic* (June):B9.

Hammond, J., P. Houston, and J. McKay. 1993. *The Religious Right: Beliefs, Goals, and Strategies—A Guide for Public School Administrators.* Summit, NJ: Horace Mann League.

Kaul, D. 1994. "Bashing Our President Is a Sport," *The Des Moines Register* (June):11-A.

Krasky, S. 1994. "Dole Comes out Jewell Teas Winner at Iowa Convention," *The Kansas City Star* (June):A-19.

Merrow, J. 1994. " 'Don't Offend': Our High-Level Policy of Cowardice," *Education Week*, 56:42.

O'Neill, B. 1994. "History of a Hoax," *Church and State*, 47(4):17–20.

Simonds, R. 1993. *President's Report*. Costa Mesa, CA: National Association of Christian Educators/Citizens for Excellance in Education, p. 3.

INDEX

AIDS, 6, 117–118
ALEXANDER, LAMAR, 82, 89, 126
ALLEN, JEANNE, 17–19
American Association of School Administrators (AASA), 81, 116
American Center for Law and Justice, 7
American Coalition for Traditional Values, 35
American conservatism, 67–68
American Federation of Teachers (AFT), 82
American Spectator, 68
ANDERSON, JILL, 39

BATES, STEVEN, 3, 16, 21
BELL, TERRELL H., 89–90
BENNETT, WILLIAM, 18, 77–78, 82, 89–90, 117, 138
BLOOM, BEN, 10–11
BRACEY, GEORGE, 74–75, 106
BRINKLEY, ALAN, 67
BROOKHISER, RICHARD, 28
BUCHANAN, PAT, 126–127
BUSH, GEORGE, 17, 27, 32, 43, 85, 87–89, 110

California Proposition 174, 74–75, 82
CARROLL, JOHN, 10
Catcher in the Rye, 6

CAVAZOS, LAURO, 89
CHALKER, DONALD A., 91–92
CHENEY, DICK, 126
Christian Coalition, 27, 34–37, 43–45, 62, 66, 72
Christian Right, 31–32, 34–38, 42, 49
Citizens for Excellence in Education (CEE), 35–36, 45, 51–54, 62–66, 72, 106
CLARK, RAMSEY, 117
CLINTON, PRESIDENT BILL, 27–28, 43, 87–89
Cognitive competence, 75–77
Concerned Citizens for Public Education, 106
Concerned Women for America, 16, 35, 66, 72
Condoms, 82, 118–119
Connecticut school plan, 82–83, 93–94, 113
Conservative Christian, 35
CRAIGE, BETTY JEAN, 116–117
Creationism, 7, 63–64
CUMMINS, PAUL, 103

Darwinism, 14
DAVIS, T CULLEN, 138
The Depression, 101
DEWEY, JOHN, 9, 44
DOLE, ROBERT, 129
DRIPS, JOE, 49–57

Eagle Forum, 35, 73, 125
EAKMAN, B. K., 36
Education Week, 84–85
ELDERS, DR. JOYCELYN, 138
Engel v. Vitale, 14
ENGLER, GOVERNOR, JIM, 82
Equal Access Act, 7
ESCALANTE, JAMIE, 69–70

FALWELL, JERRY, 3, 14, 31, 68
FEGE, ARNOLD, 126
FLORIO, GOVERNOR JIM, 82
Free World Research Report, 78
FROST, VICKI, 16
Fundamentalists, 1–8, 12–16, 61–62, 65, 76–78, 85, 103, 114, 123–130, 139

GABLER, MEL AND NORMA, 31
Gallup Poll, 71, 74, 82
"The Generation That Forgot God," 37
Globalism, 116–117
Goals 2000, 9, 17, 85–89, 113
Goals 2000: Educate America Act, 17, 22, 28–37, 40–45, 127
Goals-driven school reform, 70
GOODLAD, JOHN, 70–71
Government schools, 29–31, 35–37
GRAHAM, PATRICIA, 84
GRAMM, PHIL, 126
Great School Wars, 123, 132

HAYNES, RICHARD, 91–93
Heather Has Two Mommies, 27
HELMS, JESSE, 69
Heritage Foundation, 17
Holocaust, 101
Home schooling, 130–131
HOWSE, BRANNON, 38–39
HUFSTEDLER, SHIRLEY, 89–90
HUGHES, ROBERT, 68–69
HULL, JUDGE THOMAS, 16
Humanism, 15, 31
    secular humanism, 15, 44
HUNTER, MADELINE, 10, 44

Illinois program, 71
Impressions, 6–7
Iowa Business, Labor, and Education Roundtable, 107–108
Iowa Department of Education, 107–108
Iowa Plan, 61–62
Iowa School District, 48

JEFFERSON, THOMAS, 1

Kansas program, 71–72
KELLER, FRED, 10–11
KELLY, TOM, 69
KEMP, JACK, 126
Kentucky Reform Act, 70, 106–107, 135–136
KIBBEY, MICHAEL, 106
KING, RICHARD, 103

LAHAYE, TIM, 15, 16
LEO-NYQUIST, DAVID, 71
LEPLEY, WILLIAM, 35–36, 48–49, 56–57, 107
LIMBAUGH, RUSH, 12, 137–138
Littleton School District, 96–100, 113, 132–134
LOCHAAS, REVEREND PHILLIP, 115
LOHMAN, DAVID, 76–77
LUKSIK, PEG, 46–47, 61–62

MALCOLM X, 5
MALKIN, MICHELLE, 61
Mastery learning, 10–11, 44–45
Minnesota Department of Education, 8
MOEN, MATHEW, 110
MOFFET, JAMES, 21
Moral Majority, 31
Mozart v. Hawkins County Public Schools, 15
Multiculturalism, 4–5, 116–117
MURRAY, CHARLES, 119–120

A Nation at Risk, 70

National Alliance of Business, 17
National Education Association, 65–66
National Election Panel, 85
NELSON, GOVERNOR E. BENJAMIN, 85
The New Age Is Not So New, 39
New Age Religion, 7, 36, 38–44, 114–116, 126
New Right, 31–32
New York, Johnson City, 101
NEWMAN FRANK, 83
North Carolina, Gastonia, 105, 113

Odyssey Project, 105
O'HAIR, MADALYN MURRAY, 1–2
Oklahoma School District, 46
O'NEILL, BARRY, 138–139
Outcome-Based Education, 6, 8–12, 27–37, 40–49, 55–57, 63, 66–73, 76–78, 81–85, 93–106, 110–114
OVERLY, PETER, 101
OVERSTREET, HARRY AND BONANO, 110

Parents as Teachers (PAT), 30–31, 40
Pennsylvania plan, 61–62
Pennsylvania School District, 46
People for the American Way, 5, 16–18, 27, 62–63
Personalized System of Instruction, 11
Phi Delta Kappa, 71–74, 82
Philadelphia (the movie), 117–118
Politically correct, 67–68
POSTON, KEVIN, 17
Prichard Committee for Academic Excellence, 107–108
Profiles of far-right citizens' groups, 72–73
Prohibition, 13–14
Proselytism, 7–8
Public Schools Problems List, 137
Pumsey, 7

Pumsey Program, 64

Quest, 7

Rainbow Curriculum, 27, 36, 45
RAVICH, DIANE, 123
REAGAN, NANCY, 5
REAGAN, RONALD, 17
REED, RALPH, JR., 62, 73–75
Religious identity of United States Christians, 128
Religious Right, 4, 6–7, 20, 27–38, 57–58, 64–63, 70, 78–79, 108, 116, 123, 134, 136
Religious Right glossary, 33–34
RENO, JANET, 7
RENTON, KATHLEEN, 83
Republican Party, 35–36
Restructuring, school, 70–71
RILEY, RICHARD, 7, 87–89, 113
ROBERTSON, PAT, 5, 7, 27, 31, 35, 73, 126
RYAN, KERN, 123

SCHLAFLY, PHYLLIS, 5, 12, 31, 68, 103–105, 110, 125, 138
SCHEMPP, ED, 2
SCOPES, JOHN T., 13
 monkey trial, 13, 15
 Scopes v. States, 13, 15
SCOTT, EUGENIE, 7
Secular humanism, 31–32
Sex, premarital, 117–120
SHOCKLEY, WILLIAM, 5
SIMONDS, ROBERT, 5, 36, 51, 64–66, 126–127
Situation ethics, 41
Southern Baptist Sunday School Board, 118
SPADY, BILL, 8–9, 29, 46–47, 70, 93, 96, 100

THORNDIKE, EDWARD, 75–76
Time on task, 10
Total Quality Management, 40–41
True Love Waits campaign, 118

Ultraconservatives, 63–64
University eggheads, 66

VARNOM, C. J., 103
Vermont Reform Act, 82
Virginia plan, 62
Vista board, 63
VOLLMER, JAMIE, 107–110
Vouchers, 125

WALL, KAY, 83
WESTERBERG, TIM, 96, 132–135
WILL, GEORGE, 74–75
WILMON, DONALD, 5
World Class Education, 84, 89
World class schools, 91–93
Wyoming School District, 46, 93–96, 113